# GREAT MOMENTS IN
# PRO BASKETBALL

# GREAT MOMENTS IN
# PRO BASKETBALL

### BY SAM GOLDAPER

tempo
books

**GROSSET & DUNLAP**
A FILMWAYS COMPANY
Publishers • New York

*For Toby, Marci and Barry Cash*

*For Martha, Robert and Brenda*

# CONTENTS

# 1

# The Incomparable Dr. J
# and His Longest Operation

IT WAS JUST a few hours before dawn in New York and almost midnight in San Diego. The slim gathering of 2,916, a typical crowd for the troubled San Diego Conquistadors, had quickly emptied from the International Sports Arena.

In a quiet New York Nets' dressing room, Julius Erving, pro basketball's Mr. Excitement, sat rubbing his swollen, aching feet. Minutes later, one of the ball boys brought him two ice bags which he quickly applied to his feet.

"I've never seen a game like this before," said the former captain of the Nets, "and I hope I'm never in one like this again." After a short pause and a forced smile, he added, "Unless we win. It's disheartening to lose when you have put so much into it."

In a game that took three hours and ten minutes to play, Julius Erving had just been through a four-overtime American Basketball Association contest in which the Conquistadors had beaten the Nets, 176-166.

Erving had scored 63 points, a career high, and pulled down 23 of his team's 57 rebounds. Later he was to admit that he had played the last three overtime periods with a slightly twisted ankle.

Since Erving is also known as the famed "Dr. J." in basketball circles, February 14, 1975, the night of the game, has been referred to as "The Doctor's Longest Operation." It came in the eighth season of the struggling and now defunct A.B.A.

The National Basketball Association once had a six-overtime game, but that was under ancient rules, before the 24-second clock forced teams to keep shooting and moving, rather than hold the ball and stall.

Alex Groza, the Conquistador general manager during Dr. J's "longest operation," had played in that 1951 N.B.A. six-overtime game. He was a member of the Indianapolis team that defeated the Rochester Royals, 75-73.

"In each extra period," recalled Groza, "we would just stall for one shot after getting the tap."

While the N.B.A.'s six-overtime game produced a total of 18 points, in the four extra periods of the Nets-San Diego contest the teams had scored a total of 84 points.

The combined 342 points scored by the Nets and the Conquistadors that night were the most ever recorded in professional basketball. The previous A.B.A. mark was 322 points, produced in a double-overtime contest, and the N.B.A. record was 316.

A combined total of 73 personal fouls was called against the Net and San Diego players, and they grabbed a total of 132 rebounds during the 68 minutes of playing time.

During the marathon game, seven players had each accumulated six personal fouls, which in the N.B.A. would have meant compulsory expulsion from the game. Unmercifully, the A.B.A. rules were such that players did not foul out, but instead were allowed to continue to the point of exhaustion.

For the first 47 minutes of playing time it was a seesaw game in which defense on both sides was almost nonexistent. Instead, the action featured some brilliant individual play by Erving, his teammate Brian Taylor, and Bo Lamar of San Diego.

When Bill Melchionni scored a basket with 44 seconds remaining in regulation play to give the Nets a 129-124 advantage, it appeared that New York would win. But a few seconds later, Warren Jabali, who was to emerge as the dominant San Diego player, drove for the basket. He was fouled by Willie Sojourner as the ball went through the hoop. Jabali's free throw reduced the Nets' margin to three points.

Erving, who had so far played all but two minutes and was starting to show fatigue, had a chance to make a clinching basket with eight seconds left, but he missed a long shot. Thereupon, Travis Grant, who had scored 30 points, hit a 22-footer at the final buzzer. The game was tied, 129-129.

Erving poured in 12 points in the first 5-minute overtime session, but Lamar, the nation's leading major college scorer when he played backcourt at Southwestern Louisiana, helped keep the Q's ahead. It took a 12-foot jumper by Erving with seven seconds remaining to tie the game at 144-144 and send the contest into a second overtime.

With 25 seconds to play in Overtime Period II and the Nets behind by 3 points, Mike Gale stole the ball and flipped it to Erving at the 3-point line. Erving shot—and missed, one of the five 3-pointers he missed during the game. But Bill Melchionni took possession of the ball and hit from the 3-point line, sending the game into a third overtime.

Almost the same pattern developed at the end of the third overtime. This time it was Taylor who hit with a 3-pointer with 22 seconds left, and neither side could cash in on the last-ditch opportunities that presented themselves.

By the fourth overtime many of the key Nets had spent their energy. Erving, enroute to playing a record 66 minutes, had not had a rest since the second half began.

With three minutes left, the score was tied 163-163. Then Lamar, who was to score 45 points, Jabali, and Lee Davis put together a 13-1 burst before Erving scored a basket in the last two seconds of the game. The final score: 176-166, San Diego.

After the game a sportswriter quipped, "The score sounds like they were playing half-court basketball."

A weary Erving scored only one basket in the last two overtimes, but he got 16 points in the first two extra sessions, to go along with the 45 he had scored in regulation time. He took a record 51 shots and made 25.

Just watching Erving warm up in a pregame drill is worth the price of admission. He looks like a young Elgin Baylor, the former star of the Los Angeles Lakers and one of the greatest scorers in pro basketball history. Julius holds the basketball the way most people grasp a grapefruit, and he drives to the basket like no one since Connie Hawkins' glory days in the A.B.A.

Sport fans thrive on comparison, and whenever or wherever pro basketball people come together the legends of Erving's accomplishments grow.

"Baylor was the best for a longer time," said Kevin Loughery, the Net coach, who spent eleven seasons playing in the N.B.A., "but Doc is a better all-around player than Baylor was. He can do everything Baylor could do on offense, and he plays better defense.

"There are very few guys who can play all three positions," continued Loughery. "Dave DeBusschere did it. He played center a few times with the Knicks, and when he was with the Detroit Pistons earlier in his career, he played guard. John Havlicek would be too small for center. Spencer Haywood would have trouble at guard. But we have used Doc at center when Billy Paultz was hurt, and Doc did well. We haven't used him at guard too often, but if we did he'd be an All-Star guard. At center, his size might hurt him, but he's a leaper. If he was a center, he'd be right there when they picked the All-Star center."

Erving is able to do things with a basketball which may never have been seen before. He can dribble like a guard, going behind and between his legs. Given a running start, he can leap from behind the foul line some 15 feet from the basket and slam-dunk the ball.

It was just past midnight on May 11, 1974. Less than two hours before, the Nets had beaten the Utah Stars, 111-100, for the A.B.A. championship. The Nets' dressing room was quiet, still reeking from the odor of champagne that had left the floor slippery.

Almost everyone had left to celebrate the championship at a nearby Long Island restaurant.

Kevin Loughery was still drying out from his many champagne baths and Julius Erving was not yet dressed. He was disturbed that someone had taken the license plates off his white Avanti as a souvenir.

As Erving dressed his 6-foot 7-inch, 195-pound frame, which is neither skinny nor muscular, Loughery said, "There he is, pound for pound, the greatest basketball player in the game." Meaning in the world.

In the first game of that championship season Erving had scored 47 points. But two of those field goals were more amazing than any of his other shots. They came as Erving was loping around the left corner in front of the Nets' bench when he started to drive the base line. But he was being angled out of bounds by Bruce Seals, the 6-9 forward guarding him. Although far behind the plane of the backboard, Dr. J. sprang high, reached out with the ball in his right hand and flicked it over Seals' outstretched hand, past the side of the backboard and through the rim. His stunned teammates, on and off the court, snapped their heads from side to side, and in the stands the crowd shrieked.

When someone later asked Erving about the shot, he said, "You must be new around here. It was just a one-hand shot and it still counted for two points."

But to his teammates, and the fans, it was a move that they hadn't seen before.

"Every night he upstages himself," said Kevin Loughery.

Two years and two days after the Nets' first championship, there were eleven Nets in the shower at the Nassau Coliseum, champagne bottles in their hands, singing, "We're number one. We're number one." The

Nets had just won another A.B.A. title, 112-106, in a five-game series that paired Julius Erving against the Denver Nuggets.

In the opening game, which the Nets won, 120-118, the Good Doctor scored 45 points, including 18 of his team's 28 points in the final seven minutes and 43 seconds. But his most important shot came on a 20-foot baseline jumper at the buzzer that won the game.

In the first against the Nuggets, he had personally accounted for 96 points, 26 rebounds, and 12 assists. But to understand Dr. J's true greatness, you had to actually watch him in the Nets' 117-111 triumph in the third game.

With the Nets ahead, 109-108, and 1:45 left in the game, Erving did all of the following things:

● Leaped out of the crowd under the basket to make the score 111-108.

● Soared near the ionosphere to block an open shot by Bobby Jones at Denver's end of the court.

● Broke up a three-on-one fast break and then again came out of nowhere to block an open layup by Chuck Williams.

● Went one-on-one with Bobby Jones and scored on a reverse left-handed layup to make the score, 113-111, with 30 seconds left.

● Controlled the ball along the sideline for the last 15 seconds of the game, and then scored the Nets' final points with a joyous back-handed stuff.

In the five games he had scored a total of 195 points, averaged 13.2 rebounds, blocked 9 shots and stolen the ball thirteen times.

But to Erving it all seemed routine.

"I've worked in practice on every move I've ever made," Erving has often said. "Sometimes it happens when I've got the ball and the game is on the line, so what I do becomes magnified. But things that seem spontaneous really aren't. Only once in a hundred times, maybe, I'll surprise myself, come up with something I've never done before. It's all instinct on the court, but most of the things I do, like fancy dunkshots or twisting shots, I've done before in other games or practice."

It all began for Erving in Roosevelt, Long Island.

The sign on the gate reads "Roosevelt Park." This is where Erving started to do the things that have made him one of the greatest players in the game.

At nearby Roosevelt High School, a predominantly black school, the Good Doctor is a legend. Newspaper articles about his feats wallpaper the trophy case. His picture hangs in the elementary school where Earl Mosley, Erving's first coach and long-time confidante, once said, "Everybody in the entire district talks about him."

Art Flechner, the district athletic director, added, "They live and breathe his movements. He's talked about constantly."

At graduation time a few years ago, Roosevelt High did not seek out politicians or educators for their guest speaker. Instead, they went for one of their own, and brought back Julius Erving.

Erving has never forgotten the Roosevelt school district or Roosevelt Park. During the 1975-76 school year, the district ran into a financial squeeze and the athletic program faced curtailment. The school district called on its favorite son again. Julius rode the Long Island Railroad telling commuters of the school's problems and began a fund-raising drive.

After Roosevelt High School, Erving took his

greatness to the University of Massachusetts, where he remained for three years before he left to sign an A.B.A. contract with the Virginia Squires.

Erving averaged 27.3 points during his rookie A.B.A. season (1970-71) and 31.9 points the following season.

On most given nights, in any A.B.A. city, Erving treated the fans to some of his spectacular play. Some nights he was more spectacular than others.

When the A.B.A still had a franchise in Florida, Erving put on a show that made a believer out of Bob Bass, the Floridian coach, and left the crowd screaming.

"He took the whole building through the net on that one stuff shot," said Bass. "He took off from before the free-throw line and flew along in the strato. When he dunked the ball, he created such a vacuum that everyone's ears cracked on the bench."

Another time, in Kentucky, Lou Dampier of the Colonels pitched a long pass downcourt. Erving leaped, hauled the ball down with one hand, slammed it just once, catapulted back into the air, and dunked it.

Before the start of the 1972-73 season, Erving jumped to the Atlanta Hawks of the N.B.A. While the N.B.A. was hassling over whether his move to Atlanta was legal—since the Milwaukee Bucks owned Erving's draft rights—the Squires traded him to the Nets.

It was the best move the struggling Nets' franchise had made. Born as the Jersey Americans for the 1967-68 season, the Nets played their first year in the Teaneck Armory. The following season they played in the Commack (L.I.) Arena. Burst hot-water pipes, a buckled basketball floor, fans who huddled in overcoats to stay warm, and a $106,000 gross for the 42-game home schedule are all parts of the Nets' early history.

On August 1, 1973, the day Julius signed a seven-year, $1.9 million Nets' contract, almost 100 people lined up on a blistering hot day to purchase Nets' season tickets that sold at a top price of $350.

Hours after the news conference announcing his signing, Erving was back at Roosevelt Park telling people, "That's the best basket, that one there," pointing to the nearest one. "That's where I played the most."

That same day a kid asked Erving, "You really a surgeon, Doctor?"

Erving, more restrained in conversation than on the court, sat the youngster on his lap and said, "Oh, it's something I picked up in high school and it has stayed with me ever since. I had this friend, Leon Saunders, who played on our school team. I used to call him the Professor, because he always wanted to argue.

"It was then that he started calling me the Doctor. When we went to college together and he started calling me that around the dorm, all the others picked up on it.

"When I started playing in the Rucker Tournament everybody had a nickname. They called me Houdini, Black Moses, and the Claw. One day I walked over to the announcer and said, 'Look, why don't you just call me the Doctor?' The nickname stuck with the people in Harlem and everywhere else.

"After I got to Virginia I was rooming with Willie Sojourner and he expanded the name to Dr. J. I don't know why. The guys on the team call me Doc."

When Erving was finished telling his story, the

youngster smiled and said, "You really operate on those players."

Erving is a doctor of sorts, a basketball doctor, but his cures are only for the team on which he plays. His opponents become ill—with envy—when he passes the ball from his right to his left hand, pumps twice, then defies the laws of gravity before letting the ball fly forth from somewhere behind his ear.

On June 17, 1976, the A.B.A., which began as an 11-team league with the 1967-68 season and had had franchises in 22 different cities, went out of business. The New York Nets, Denver Nuggets, Indiana Pacers, and San Antonio Spurs were absorbed into the N.B.A.

Julius Erving, the A.B.A.'s Mr. Excitement, was finally in the N.B.A., and it was supposed to do wonders for the Nets.

Erving never got to play for the N.B.A. Nets. When a contract dispute developed and he refused to report to training camp, he was sold to the Philadelphia 76ers for $2.5-million.

Under the guise of team play, the Dr. J. of the Nets and the playgrounds sometimes disappeared. Erving did not have the same freedom to do what he did when he was a Net. He shot less and gave up more of his game because he was on a talent-laden team that included such offensive standouts as George McGinnis, Doug Collins, and Lloyd Free.

By midseason George McGinnis had said, "You're never going to see Dr. J. again . . . that's over." McGinnis was correct.

While the Philadelphia 76ers became the biggest road show in the league, playing only to sellouts, Erving was disappointing people every time he put his hand on a basketball. Soon they were asking, "Where's the Julius Erving everyone was talking about?"

Erving was there, but he was more professional about the game now, if not sensational. During a time-out he would say, "Let's run this play. Let's get George open here." Or, "Hey, I think I can beat that guy." He was not selfish.

But every once in a while the real Julius Erving would emerge. Like in the 1977 All-Star Game when he was voted the most valuable player. In 30 minutes of playing time he collected 30 points, 13 in the fourth quarter. Three of his 12 baskets were dunk shots. On his first dunk he beat Rick Barry of the Golden State Warriors down the floor, went down the lane, and jammed the ball through the hoop over 7-2 Kareem Abdul-Jabbar. The play brought the capacity crowd to their feet. At least for the moment, Dr. J had returned.

# 2

# Wilt's 100-Point Night

O.J. SIMPSON, pro football's premier running back, once remarked, "I only live a few miles away from Wilt, but I find I'm farther away than I thought."

Simpson, who owned a $100,000 home near the San Diego Freeway, made the statement at a giant 1972 party Wilt Chamberlain threw for his friends to show off his new $1.5-million mansion, built on a two-acre site overlooking Bel Air from the front and the San Fernando Valley from the back.

The entrance to the house has a 14-foot-high, 1,500 pound door that swings open as if by magic. The master bedroom has a 72-square-foot bed, which was covered by a bedspread made from "wolf-nose" fur cut from pelts he purchased from Alaska bounty hunters. There is a 280-gallon bathtub of golden mosaic tile and a bathroom specially designed for a man who is 7 feet tall. It has six shower heads that can spray Wilt at every angle from the mirrored wall.

Wilt Chamberlain always did things in a big way. Like when he left the University of Kansas after his junior year to join the Harlem Globetrotters, Chamberlain made the announcement in a national magazine. Like the 31,419 points and 23,924 rebounds he accumulated in his fourteen pro seasons playing in Philadelphia, San Francisco, and Los Angeles.

In the "All-Time Select Circle" pages of the *National Basketball Association Guide,* the league record book, more than two pages are devoted to Chamberlain's record-breaking feats. Many of them were recorded on that memorable night of March 2, 1962, when Wilt scored his 100 points against the New York Knicks in Hershey, Pennsylvania.

During the 1961-62 season, his third in the N.B.A., the 270-pound Chamberlain scored 50 or more points in 46 of the eighty games on the Philadelphia schedule and finished with a 50.4 season average.

Chamberlain began his onslaught on the record book on December 8, 1961, in Philadelphia when he broke the all-time single-game scoring record by collecting 78 points in a triple-overtime contest against the Lakers. On January 13, 1962, he tallied 73 points against Chicago and broke the mark of 71 points for a regulation game held by Elgin Baylor of Los Angeles.

Baylor greeted Wilt's record-breaking performance with this prediction: "Some day soon somebody is going to score a hundred points in a game. There is no ceiling, except time, on how many points a man can score."

Baylor was not the only one to predict a 100-point game mark. Oscar Robertson, playing for the Cincinnati Royals at the time, had also stated that Wilt would hit the century mark in a game, after Chamberlain had his 78-point night.

At the time Robertson said, "There is no telling how many points Wilt can get. I wouldn't be surprised to see him get a hundred."

And Easy Ed MacAuley, playing for the St. Louis Hawks, agreed with Robertson and Baylor when he said, "He can score anything he wants. There is no way to stop him. How can you defense him? The only way I know is to lock the door of the dressing room before he comes out."

During the 1961-62 season, the N.B.A. was a nine-team league. It had not yet tasted the expansion boom that would bring the league membership to twenty-two teams for the 1976-77 season with the admission of four teams from the defunct American Basketball Association. Nor had the N.B.A. yet received the national television exposure and the big monies derived from TV that it enjoys today. Also, in the struggling years of the N.B.A. it was a common practice for teams, seeking more national exposure for the sport, to play in cities away from their regular home bases.

As the Philadelphia Warriors pulled into Hershey, they were greeted by a huge sign: "Welcome to Chocolate Town." Little did the 4,124 people who came to the tiny arena that night realize they would witness the greatest offensive show in the history of basketball.

In compiling his incredible 100 points, Chamberlain took 63 shots and made 36 and sank 28 of 32 free throws as the Warriors routed the hapless Knicks, buried in last place, 160-147. Strangely, the 28 free throws were a great feat by Wilt, who had a history of not being a very good free-throw shooter. He averaged about 60 percent during the early days of his career and slipped to 38 percent during the 1966-67 season, his last in Philadelphia.

As the teams took position for the start of the game, Darrall Imhoff, 6-10, 220 pounds, the Knick center, faced Chamberlain for the tipoff. Following referee Willie Smith's whistle, the ball went up in the air and Wilt tapped it to Guy Rodgers, the Warriors' small, swift backcourt man. Rodgers dribbled the ball a while to give his team a chance to set up the offense. He then passed off quickly to Paul Arizin. who leaped, shot from the corner, and missed. Chamberlain reached up, brought down the rebound, and dunked it for his first basket.

Before the Knicks knew what had hit them, Chamberlain had quickly collected 13 points, including seven successive free throws, and the Warriors were off to a 19-3 advantage. At the end of the first quarter, Chamberlain had hit on half of his 14 attempts and made nine free throws. The warriors led, 42-26, and Wilt had collected 23 of the points.

During the next quarter, Chamberlain banked in jump shots over Imhoff's strained hand, bulled his way through the defense to stuff rebounds with his frightening jump shot, and slipped in his underhand shot. Once or twice he even raced downcourt to follow up shots after the fast break.

Imhoff was later to say, "He was so strong that he was picking us up and stuffing us through the hoop along with the ball. We tried collapsing three men around him, but it didn't help. He was getting downcourt so fast that night, I couldn't keep up with him."

During the second quarter he had added 18 more

points to bring his total to 41 as the Warriors led, 79-68. He made seven of his twelve field-goal attempts.

In the Warrior dressing room, Frank McGuire, the Philadelphia coach at the time, told his team, "Wilt is getting free underneath, let's keep getting the ball to him."

It was opposite to the strategy Eddie Donovan, in his first season as the Knick coach, was trying to convey to his team. He tried to impress on the Knicks that they had to stop the other Warriors from getting the ball in to Wilt. Actually, the Knicks had little chance since Imhoff was in foul trouble and Donovan had been forced to use 6-7 Cleveland Buckner at center.

The second half began with Wilt bringing his total to 45 points on two quick field goals. He added another on a short jumper, and then Rodgers passed to him under the basket. He turned, leaped up, and forced the ball into the basket as Imhoff—whom Donovan had sent back in—fouled him. As Chamberlain hit the free throw, the announcer said, "That was Chamberlain's fiftieth point," and the crowd responded with a deafening roar.

Wilt had made 10 of his 16 shots in the third quarter as his dunks and fallaway jumpers were going through the basket almost uncontested. Going into the final 12 minutes, the Warriors held a 125-106 lead, and Wilt had scored 69 points.

By now the Warriors, sensing a record, began working seriously at feeding the ball to Chamberlain. Wilt spun and scored on a layup under Buckner's arm, followed with a dunk shot and on a fallaway jumper. With 10 minutes and 10 seconds left to play, he slammed in a rebound to bring his total to 75 points.

Donovan sent Imhoff back into the game again, but

he fouled out and that made the Knicks' chances to contain Chamberlain even tougher. With 7:51 showing on the clock, Rodgers got a pass into Wilt at the foul line and he hit on a one-hander for his 79th point.

As the clock began to tick away, the crowd began to chant, "Give it to Wilt! Give it to Wilt! Give it to Wilt!"

At the 5-minute mark, Al Attles, currently the coach of the Golden State Warriors, who hadn't missed a shot in eight attempts, passed by an easy shot and instead fed the ball to Chamberlain. Wilt leaped high over the rim and rammed the ball through the shaking cords for his 89th point.

In an effort to avoid embarrassment, Donovan ordered his team to use as much of the 24-second clock as possible before taking a shot. The Knicks also began fouling the other Warriors in order to keep Wilt from getting the ball.

McGuire countered the Knick strategy by sending York Larese, Joe Ruklick, and Ted Luckenbill, his substitutes, into the game with orders to foul the Knicks as soon as they got the ball. This hurt the Knicks' ability to stall and got the ball to the Warriors, who in turn set-up Wilt.

Chamberlain did not score again until only 2:45 remained. Then he made a foul shot, added two more free throws, and connected for a fadeaway jumper. He now had 94 points.

With the Warriors again in possession, Rodgers dribbled the ball over midcourt, faked his way by a Knick defender, and whipped the ball to Wilt. It bounced out of Chamberlain's hands, but the big giant recovered it and flipped in a jumper for his 96th point.

Again the Knicks tried to freeze the ball but it got

loose. Larese picked it up and moved it into the frontcourt. Meanwhile Wilt had positioned himself near the basket. Larese lofted a high pass to Wilt and he dunked it for his 98th point with 1:19 remaining.

The Knicks tried to pass the ball in bounds, but it was intercepted by Chamberlain who shot a one-hander from the foul line. The ball hit the rim and bounced off.

The Knicks brought the ball downcourt and missed a shot. The Warriors grabbed the rebound and Ruklick fed the ball to Chamberlain in the pivot. Wilt shot and missed, grabbed the rebound, shot and missed again. Luckenbill outfought the Knicks for the rebound, and passed it to Ruklick as the clock kept running. Suddenly, Ruklick spotted Wilt under the basket and lobbed the ball to Chamberlain. In one sweeping motion Wilt leaped high, clamped both hands on the ball, and stuffed it through the hoop for his 100th point!

Forty-six seconds still remained in the game as the announcer's voice was lost in the din of the crowd. Paper cups and newspapers were thrown on the floor and some two hundred people rushed to the court to touch and shake his hand. Even the Knicks joined in the congratulatory excitement.

"Thank you, thank you," said Chamberlain over and over again as the police tried in vain to pull the people away from him.

It took a total of nine minutes before the last seconds of the game could be completed.

"Tonight," said McGuire, who went on to become coach of the University of South Carolina, "was a wonderful thrill. I can remember the first time a team I coached scored a hundred points. That was a great moment. Now this. It's almost unbelievable."

In the Warrior dressing room, Arizin stood shaking his head in disbelief. "I never thought I would see it happen when I came into this league. It's a fantastic thing to be part of."

Rodgers, who had 20 assists, said, "There was no easier way in the world to get an assist tonight. All I had to do was give the ball to the Dipper."

Attles, who had a perfect night from the field with eight baskets, likes to talk about that game.

"I remember telling the big fella," said Attles, "I'll have a mental block for the rest of my life. I don't miss a shot and nobody even talks to me."

Meanwhile, on the bus ride back to New York, Imhoff sat alone in deep thought. Finally, he looked up, shook his head, and said, "I can't have a nightmare tonight. I've just lived through one."


To watch Chamberlain on the basketball court, or the dance floor, was a thing of beauty. As one of the world's greatest athletes, his reflexes were magnificent and his sense of timing superb. In short, he was pro basketball's incomparable superstar and one of the most commanding figures in the history of the sport.

His hands from the tip of his middle finger to the break of his wrist, measured 9½ inches. He could reach 9 feet, 6 inches into the air standing flatfooted, and with a couple of steps and a leap he could reach 12 feet 6 inches.

The thing that Chamberlain hated most was to be considered a freak. At various times he contemplated leaving basketball to become a professional decathlon star. He had even listened to offers to play pro football for the Kansas City Chiefs and to box professionally. People who knew him best said he was always trying to prove that he was an outstanding athlete, that his height had nothing to do with becoming a basketball great.

"Wilt would have been better off," Alex Hannum, one of his many pro coaches, once said, "if he never got beyond six-eleven. I think it would have made all the difference in the world in his personality. It's like he always said, 'Who ever felt sorry for Goliath?' "

The basketball world began hearing about Chamberlain at the age of 16 when he was a student at Overbrook High School in Philadelphia—and had already grown to 6 feet, 11 inches.

"The big difference between Wilt and just another tall boy was that he was coordinated and agile," Sam Cozen, his coach at Overbrook, once said. "He had huge hands, and he knew all the tricks and angles in rebounding. He had great stamina, too. He could run all day and never get tired. But when we first got him he was as green as grass. But he did have a pretty close-in hook and a fadeaway shot, and he was a better foul shooter in high school than he was in the pros.

"He scored in the twenties and thirties, but we had to teach him aggressiveness. In those days the biggest boy he'd face was six-four, and he had the narrow center lanes to help him, too."

On November 27, 1955, with Chamberlain still in high school, the N.B.A. owners, in an unprecedented move, granted the Philadelphia Warriors the draft rights to Wilt when his college class graduated. (In high school he led Overbrook to three league and two city titles and scored a record 2,252 points.)

The late Joe Lapchick, then the Knick coach, protested the decision. "The league created a monster when they gave Chamberlain to Philadelphia," said Lapchick. "It was a grave error."

Meanwhile, more than 100 cash-on-the line offers from colleges around the country poured in as Wilt made expense-free cross-country trips to Oregon, Dayton, Denver, Cincinnati, Illinois, Michigan, Michigan State, Iowa, Northwestern, and Kansas. Wilt finally chose to attend Kansas.

Normally, a freshman-varsity game is meaningless, but with Chamberlain playing for the Jayhawk yearlings, a crowd of 14,000 showed up, including coaches from all over the nation.

Before long the audience knew what they could expect once Wilt became a sophomore and eligible to play for the varsity. Wilt drove to the top of the key and went up for what appeared to be a one-handed jumpshot—but he didn't come down. Instead, he floated through the air, did a complete twist, and *then* scored! He wound up scoring 42 points, while being double- and triple-teamed.

More than 15,000 fans turned out for Chamberlain's first varsity game at the start of the 1956-57 season. Wilt didn't disappoint anyone. Kansas beat Northwestern, 87-69, and Chamberlain scored 52 points and grabbed 31 rebounds.

Right after his first game, the N.C.A.A. changed its rules and made it illegal for the foul shooter to cross the foul line until the ball hit either the rim or the backboard. It also legislated against a player guiding a teammate's shot into the basket. Today this is known as offensive goaltending. Both rules were directed at stopping Chamberlain.

The new legislation did little to stop Wilt, nor did his opponent's strategy of double- and triple-teaming him.

During his junior season, Wilt was continuously harassed by slow-down tactics that made him unhappy. Then, on June 10, 1958, he announced to the world that he was quitting college because the kind of basketball played was "hurting my chances of ever developing into a successful professional basketball player."

In the middle of that summer, Chamberlain joined the Harlem Globetrotters who, with their clowning, fancy dribbling, and trick plays, were the most famous barnstorming basketball team in the world. Wilt played guard on the team, and it was a great selling point to the fans who were eager to see him dribble, pass, and score.

In October, Wilt played his first game in Madison Square Garden as a Globetrotter, and more than 18,000 people came out to watch him. A Garden official said at the time, "We had so many requests for tickets we could have sold out Yankee Stadium."

In April of 1959, Wilt's contract with the Globetrotters ran out and he joined the Philadelphia Warriors. Philadelphia had long needed a big man of Wilt's stature. They also needed a box-office attraction. The Warriors had finished in last place the previous season.

The Warriors' long wait for Wilt was not in vain. Wilt's first game was against the Knicks before another capacity crowd of more than 18,000 at Madison Square Garden.

And as he was to do so many more times during his career, he harassed the Knicks with a 43-point performance. He made 17 of his 20 shots, grabbed 28 rebounds, and blocked 17 shots.

Chamberlain played three seasons in Philadelphia and then accompanied the franchise in its move to San

Francisco for the 1962-63 season. During the All-Star Game on January 15, 1965, Chamberlain was traded back to Philadelphia, where the 76ers were a new N.B.A. entry.

But in the end, Chamberlain became a luxury the 76ers could not afford, and he was traded to the Los Angeles Lakers for the 1968-69 season.

In his first season with the Lakers, one in which Jack Kent Cooke, the wealthy Los Angeles owner, tried to buy a championship with the teaming of Chamberlain with Jerry West and Elgin Baylor, Wilt said, "I've played a different game the last four or five seasons. My role continuously changed. It was that of a stopper. I was supposed to score big on some nights, and on others I was asked to play defense and sometimes just hand off. In short, I was supposed to lend a hand where the team needed help the most. It's not always easy to do that. You can't turn scoring on and off. You don't keep the touch and moves you need to go to the basket when you are only using them off and on."

Needless to say, the Lakers did not win the championship that season, and Cooke was to find out that titles are usually not bought but won on the court by team play, rather than individual superstars.

The Lakers, who had been in the final round eight of the previous eleven seasons, finally won a championship with Chamberlain adding the crowning touches.

Bill Russell, the Boston Celtic coach at the time, paid Chamberlain, once his arch-enemy on the court, a great tribute when he said, "Wilt is playing better than I used to—passing off, coming out to set up screens, picking up guys outside, and sacrificing himself for team play."

The season began with a new Laker coach, Bill Sharman, and a new Wilt Chamberlain. He was the new team captain and he took his job seriously. He was no longer the team's top scorer, but instead the top rebounder in the league and one of the assist leaders. It didn't bother Chamberlain that he scored 3 points in a game and that he was the Lakers' fourth best scorer with a 14.8 average in contrast to a career mark of 33.1 points.

More important to Wilt was to clear the backboards, flip the outlet pass to a streaking guard, and get the Laker fast break in motion.

After 14 N.B.A. seasons, the 38-year-old Chamberlain jumped from the Lakers to the San Diego Conquistadors of the now-defunct American Basketball Association, where he signed a three-year contract worth $1.8-million and received part ownership of the Q's.

The A.B.A. had hoped that Chamberlain's playing presence would raise attendance. He never got to play for the Q's, however, and instead was their coach for one season.

The Lakers had contested the jump in the courts and Chamberlain was forbidden from playing because the court had ruled that he owed Los Angeles the option year of a $450,000-a-year contract.

During Chamberlain's controversial and stormy career, in which he had been accused of having a hand in the dismissal of three of his coaches, he scored 31,419 points, grabbed 23,924 rebounds, and probably missed more free-throw attempts than the total points accumulated by most players. He was the most valuable player four times, won ten rebounding titles, and had

the distinction of never having fouled out in any of the
more than 1,200 games he had played.

### WILT'S INCREDIBLE NIGHT

Most points, one game — 100
Most field goals, one game — 36
Most free throws, one game — 28
Most shots, one game — 63
Most field goals, one half — 22
Most points, one half — 59
Most shots, one half — 37
Most points, one quarter — 31
Most shots, one quarter — 21

# 3

# The Longest Game

PRO BASKETBALL'S features and faces are ever-changing.

The 24-second clock gave the game a new dimension and interest. So did the way Bill Russell played center for the Boston Celtics. The Knicks introduced a helping offense and defense for their 1969-70 championship. And who would have thought that during the 1975-76 season Calvin Murphy of the Houston Rockets, at 5 feet 9 inches the smallest player in the National Basketball Association, would make fifty-eight successive free throws and break Bill Sharman's 1956 mark? But even Murphy's record lasted only one season. During the first weeks of the 1976-77 season, Rick Barry of the Golden State Warriors hit on 60 consecutive free throws.

Records and feats once thought untouchable continue to fall. Every time a youngster bounces a basketball on his way to school, potential talent appears to improve. But there is one feat from pro basketball's dark ages that is probably destined to live forever—the six-overtime game between the Rochester Royals and the Indianapolis Olympians on January 6, 1951.

That 1950-51 season began with 11 teams, including such long-forgotten franchises as Minneapolis, Rochester, Syracuse, Indianapolis, Baltimore, Ft. Wayne, and Tri-Cities. After 35 games, the Washington Capitals had dropped out of the league. The New York Knicks, Philadelphia, and Boston made up the other teams in the league.

In 1951 the N.B.A. was still three years away from the April 22, 1954 owners' meeting at which Danny Biasone of the Syracuse Nationals would propose the 24-second shooting clock that would revolutionize the game. The pros' struggle for recognition then was overshadowed by college basketball. For the 1950-51 season, Madison Square Garden, which owned the Knicks, managed to squeeze in only eighteen dates for its team. Four of them involved doubleheaders.

By comparison there were twenty-eight regular-season college doubleheaders scheduled at the Garden, and the "circuit" was going full-blast in Boston, Chicago, Cleveland, Buffalo, Philadelphia, and San Francisco.

Artistically, the Rochester Royals, made up of players from Eastern colleges, were quick, rather than big and smart. They played give-and-go. They were good set shooters and slick, opportunistic ball handlers. They believed in team play.

Most of the other team rosters were composed of players from Midwestern colleges. They were more physical, bigger, stronger, and more suited for the contact game.

Bob Davies, a first-team All-Star, and Bobby Wanzer made up the starting backcourt for Rochester. They could both hit from the outside and drive. Davies was a great ball handler, dribbler, and behind-the-back passer, and because of his talents the Royals utilized ball control.

Ben Kerner, the former owner of the old St. Louis Hawks, once said, "Bob Davies was the best backcourt man I knew. His partner, Bobby Wanzer, was a great player, too."

Speed was not an important ingredient in the Rochester attack. The plays revolved around Arnie Risen, the high-scoring 6-9 center. Although not as overpowering under the boards as George Mikan of the Minneapolis Lakers would have been, Risen knew how to handle the ball.

Red Holzman and Pep Saul were the backup guards, and Jack Coleman (6-7) and Arnie Johnson (6-5) were strong and versatile corner men. The other players on the roster were Paul Noel, Bill Calhoun, and Bill McNamee.

The Rochester Royals had a distinct personality, but none of the players had as much as Les Harrison, their owner-coach and general manager.

The ownerships typical of a quarter of a century ago are quickly disappearing. The individual sportsman, the wealthy gentleman who would support a team as a hobby and for the good of the game, has been replaced by conglomorates, public-stock ownerships, and partnerships that sometimes include as many as 100 people.

Harrison was one of the "office-in-my-hat" owners

who made pro basketball so colorful in those days. There are some who said he lacked refinement—especially while screaming at the officials. But he knew basketball and he knew how to combine scheming with a small budget to keep his team alive. He and his brother Jack ran the club, scouted, attended owners' meetings, counted the house and the receipts, served as ticket-takers, and found time to play poker with newspapermen.

The Indianapolis Olympians became a pro franchise for the 1949-50 season. The team revolved around Cliff Barker, the player coach, Alex Groza, Joe Holland, Ralph Beard, and "Wah Wah" Jones. All had played together for the University of Kentucky for four seasons following World War II, when no college team could match the mighty Wildcats. They had won two N.C.A.A. titles and one National Invitation Tournament during that span.

Allowing the Olympians into the league had to be one of the strangest expansions in N.B.A. history—or in the history of any sport. The other N.B.A. owners, swayed by the reputations of the former Kentucky standouts and hopeful they would provide some instant drawing power, let the team into the league intact.

Each player had a piece of the club. Today, players are rarely given even a share of a team's ownership.

"I remember," said Red Holzman, who was the Royals' co-captain, "when we used to come to Indianapolis. There was a guy out there who owned a store. Klautz, I think his name was. They used to call the team the Indianapolis Klautz's, or something like that. We'd play there and then head back to Rochester. On the way we would stop and play a game as the Schenectady Royals and pick up some extra money.

The next night we would play in Rochester as the Rochester Royals. I made a lot of money in those days—four hundred dollars a month."

Today the average N.B.A. salary is well over $100,000.

The six-overtime game was played at the Edgerton Sports Arena in Rochester, a cozy stadium with a capacity of 5,000, including standees. The crowd watching the 78 minutes of basketball that night numbered 3,300.

Red Holzman, who in 1967 became the coach of the Knicks, recalled that historic Rochester game. "We lost to Indianapolis, and I think I played all but two minutes. We didn't lose much at home. There was no twenty-four-second clock in those days. Each team would get the ball and hold it. It was discipline."

Holzman was correct about his playing time in the game; he played 76 minutes, 28 more than in a normal game. He scored 3 points and had seven assists in the game the Olympians won, 75-73.

The game was filled with numerous climactic plays. At the end of the regulation play the teams were deadlocked at 65-65. In two of the six overtime periods there was no scoring at all; the teams froze the ball trying for the last shot. In one of the extra sessions neither team managed to get a shot off.

In the fifth overtime, Arnie Risen accounted for both of the Royals' baskets. The first basket came when Risen, halted by Groza, somehow sneaked around Alex for a layup. Then, after Beard had tallied for the Olympians, Risen scored on a frantic hook shot.

In the final extra session, the Royals controlled the ball for three and one-half minutes. With the score

73-73, Harrison called a timeout to discuss the upcoming strategy.

After the timeout, the Olympians forced the Royals into a desperation shot, and then a frantic tap-in—which failed. Groza grabbed the rebound and got it out to Paul Walther, who threw it three-quarters of the length of the court to Beard, who was standing near the foul circle. After dribbling once, Beard tossed the ball in a high arc through the hoop with one second remaining, ending a seven-game Rochester winning streak.

"I doubt that [such overtime marathons] will ever happen again," said Holzman. "The twenty-four-second clock forces a team to shoot, and don't forget the shooters today are great. It's very tough for two teams to keep tying in overtime periods. Something has to give."

"If there had been a twenty-four-second clock," recalled Les Harrison, "the game would never have gone six overtimes. In fact, our team, with Holzman, Davies, and Wanger, were all great ball handlers and playmakers, and they were very much responsible for the advent of the twenty-four-second clock.

"Red Holzman was one of my key men that year. He could dribble the ball indefinitely, and when the other team fouled him trying to get the ball, Red proved himself to be an excellent foul shooter."

Frank Baumholtz recalled the 1941 National Invitation Tournament at Madison Square Garden that had matched him against Holzman. Baumholtz played for Ohio University and Holzman for City College.

"It was a real head-to-head duel," Baumholtz said. "Red was a tough defensive player, a typical New York ball player, a good ball handler and very smart."

Nat Holman, Holzman's college coach, commenting on Baumholtz's statement, said, "That's a fair evaluation of Bill." Holman always called Holzman "Bill," never Red.

"He was a good player even when I got him," remembered Holman. "A good floor man, a team man, and a very dependable player. He was always easygoing and even-tempered and had a good sense of humor. He had a certain amount of leadership qualities, so it didn't really surprise me when he ended up as a coach. My greatest recollection of Bill as a player was that he was excellent on defense, and I would always put him on the opposition's best player, and Bill would put the saddle on him."

Holzman played ten seasons in the N.B.A. They still tell the story of his desire to beef up the thin body he carried in order to compete against the muscle men of the league. He roomed with Fuzzy Levane and the late Dolly King. Every morning, he watched in wonder when King, the big man, would put a raw egg in a glass of sherry and drink it down.

"It helps build a strong body," King would explain to Holzman. So Red tried it out one morning.

"Maybe," Red says, grinning, "that's why I turned to drinking beer on the rocks."

The pro rules then were substantially different from what they are now.

"You could dribble with two hands then," said Holzman, "and a good ball handler could hold the ball for five minutes, maybe more."

Holzman learned from Nat Holman, Les Harrison, and from Bob Pettit, one of pro basketball's all-time greats. Holzman was Pettit's first pro coach when he began an outstanding eleven-season career in 1954 with the Milwaukee Hawks.

It was the experience that Holzman gained as a player, scout, and coach that enabled him to become perhaps the leading exponent of team basketball. True, the game has undergone some drastic changes since those days. The two-handed set shot has been replaced by jump shots, hook shots, and driving layups. There are big forwards and small forwards, penetrating guards and wing men. The running game is the "in" thing today, but the concept of helping team offenses and defenses, brought into the forefront by Holzman's coaching, will always be a coach's ultimate goal.

Holzman went into coaching retirement after the 1976-77 season. The game the way he played it that January 6, 1951 night in Rochester, is hardly recognizable today, but the six-overtime game and Holzman, have found enduring places in the great moments of pro basketball history.

# 4

# The Silver Anniversary Team

OVER THE YEARS, pro basketball has become more physical, and the players have become bigger, stronger, and quicker. George Mikan, the tall, immobile center, was followed by Bill Russell, who introduced an intimidating defense to the pivot. Then came Wilt Chamberlain, the stationary pivot who depended on ball handing and muscle. He, in turn, was followed by Kareem Abdul-Jabbar and Dave Cowens.

Abdul-Jabbar, 7-2, is the moving pivot with the speed and the shooting touch of a forward. Cowens, 6-8½, a 230-pound left-hander, has shown that speed can neutralize, even overcome, a height disadvantage. Cowens runs on every play. He's all over the court. He switches out. He plays defense. In fact, he's been described as "an animal" under the boards.

No longer does a forward need to be big and strong. Nowadays, with the increased speed and the fast break, every roster includes a "small" forward, the likes of John Havlicek of the Boston Celtics, Jim McMillian of the Buffalo Braves, Mike Riordon of the Washington Bullets, and the recently retired Bill Bradley of the Knicks. All are in 6-4, 6-5 range.

The backcourt, too, has been revolutionized and specialized. There are big and small guards—playmakers, shooters, passers, defensive specialists, and penetrators.

During its silver anniversary year, 1971, the National Basketball Association stopped, looked back, and paid tribute to its past, in celebration of one of pro basketball's greatest moments.

On January 12, 1971, at the 21st Annual All-Star Game in San Diego, the N.B.A. turned back the clock and selected the 10 greatest retired stars of its first quarter century. Also selected was Red Auerbach as the Silver Anniversary coach.

The historic occasion brought back memories of Bob Davies' ball handling before the institution of the 24-second clock, Joe Fulks' introduction of the jump shot, Bob Cousy's style of play, the feats of Bill Russell, Paul Arizin's ability to hang at the top of his jump shot, and the inspired play of Bob Pettit.

Here, in retrospect, is a look at the Silver Anniversary team and its coach:

## ARNOLD (RED) AUERBACH

During his twenty coaching seasons, Red Auerbach, current president and general manager of the Boston Celtics, was called a dictator, a tactician, a genius, a referee-baiter, and a frustrated actor.

The late Walter Brown hired Auerbach, who had previously coached the Washington Capitals and Tri-

Cities, to take over as coach of the Boston Celtics for the 1950-51 season. The Celtics were a team in trouble. Through his uncanny trading and workhorse training tactics, Auerbach rebuilt the Celtics from cellar-dweller to the most famous pro basketball dynasty in history.

With the addition of Bill Russell in 1957, the Celtics won their first N.B.A. championship. And two years later, they began a string of nine straight titles, a feat unequaled in professional athletics.

Like Leo Durocher, the famed baseball manager who once said, "Nice guys finish last," Auerbach wrapped up his winning philosophy in a slogan. As he drove the Celtics relentlessly forward he would often say, "Show me a good loser, and I'll show you a loser."

### PAUL ARIZIN
(Philadelphia Warriors 1951-52 through 1961-62)

- Won scoring championships in 1951-52 with a 25.4 average and in 1956-57 with 25.6
- A nine-time All-Star and the M.V.P. in the 1951-52 game
- At 6-4, he played the forward at a time when theoretically the frontcourt was reserved for the bruising 6-7, 6-8, and 6-9 players
- Had a career scoring average of 22.8 points
- Was the fifth player in N.B.A. history to reach the 10,000-point mark, and had a single-game career high of 44 points

An asthmatic, with an uncanny ability to "hang" at the top of his jump shot, Paul Arizin would run down the court gulping for air, the unruly cowlick on the back of his head flopping up and down. He usually headed for the corner, took a pass, faked, jumped, and hung suspended in the air for a split second before firing his line-drive shot home.

Paul Arizin developed his trademark, that spectacular jump shot, by accident while playing in the Catholic Club League in Philadelphia. "Our games were on slick dance floors," he said. "When I tried to hook, my feet would go out from under me. So I jumped. The ceiling was low and I had to throw line drives. I just never changed."

A Philadelphia sportswriter, describing the perfection of Arizin's jump shot, once wrote: "Flicking the ball on the crest of his leap like a man riding an invisible surf, this was Arizin's moment of expression."


### BOB COUSY

(Boston Celtics 1950-51 through 1962-63)
● Most Valuable Player, 1956-57
● Led the league in assists for nine successive seasons
● Played on six Boston Celtic championship teams
● Scored 1,000 or more points for thirteen consecutive seasons
● Played in thirteen consecutive All-Star games
● Named coach of the Cincinnati Royals in 1969.


Bob Cousy has meant a lot of things to different people. To the late Walter Brown, who owned the Boston Celtics, Cousy personified success. "He made professional basketball in Boston," Brown often said.

To youngsters everywhere, Cousy was once the symbol of the best basketball style. In widely scattered school yards or playgrounds, youngsters were forever trying to copy Cousy's unique style and his behind-the-back dribble. Usually, when a youngster failed to emulate the man they called "The Houdini of the Hardwood," some onlooker would cry out, "Who do you think you are—Bob Cousy?"

By build, temperament, and vision Cousy was equipped to dazzle. Although he was short for basketball (6-1½), his arms were disproportionately long, which helped him pass behind his back. His hands were big and powerful, and that helped him control the ball. His forte was playmaking, though he was also an excellent scorer.

The spectator could never anticipate Cousy's next move. The ball might go anywhere, behind his back, between his legs, nobody ever knew. Bill Sharman, his backcourt mate for a time, once said, "The first time we played together he bounced a pass off my head. He looks one way, feints a second, and passes a third. He bounced quite a few off my head before I adjusted. It was a continual adjustment—that he could hit me with a perfect pass when I didn't think one was possible."

### BOB DAVIES
(Rochester Royals 1945-46 through 1954-55)
- While playing with the Rochester Royals he also coached Seton Hall University to a 24-3 record
- An All-League selection four times
- N.B.A. assist leader, 1948-49
- Played on 1950-51 championship Rochester Royal team.

The Bob Davies-Bob Wanzer duo was looked upon as the top guard combination to play in the N.B.A. in the pre-24-second clock era. Together they made the Rochester Royals the top team of their time. Davies was one of the few guards who received recognition in the days of the tall, immobile center who would station himself under the basket and stay there until he got the ball.

Although Bob Cousy made the behind-the-back dribble famous, it was Davies who invented the trick dribble. Along with Wanzer he got the Royals to run a fast break. The 6-1 Davies was the playmaker who would set up Wanzer, who could gird a complete team from the outside when left unguarded.

Davies could throw the opposition off-balance with his trick dribbles and he saved them for just the right spot. He had a flair for the dramatic, and his dribble dazzlers usually came in a one-on-one situation with the outcome of the game hanging in the balance.

Nat Holman, a member of the Original Celtics and the coach at City College, once said, "Davies is equally as good anywhere on the court. His change-of-pace dribble is the best and the trickiest there is. Davies is a team man, setting up plays and acting as a leader."

### JOE FULKS

(Philadelphia Warriors 1946-47 through 1953-54)

- Credited with introducing the jump shot into pro basketball
- Led league in scoring with a 23.2 average, a spectacular feat in its time
- Scored 63 points on February 10, 1949, against Indianapolis, a league record that stood for more than a decade
- Played for the 1946-47 championship Philadelphia Warriors

- Named to three All-League teams; played in two All-Star games.

Joe Fulks was the link between pre-war days and the modern era of pro basketball. Before the arrival of the slim 6-5, 190-pound Fulks, basketball was not considered a high-scoring game. Fulks changed that and many other aspects of play—his twisting pivot shots were the forerunner of the jump shot.

In March of 1976 Fulks was murdered. In the period of mourning that followed, many veterans recalled his contribution to basketball. Matt Guokas, who played with him on the Warriors, said, "If there is one player who revolutionized the game, it was Joe Fulks. He came from the Marines to the big city and became a star. This might have been the first big city he was ever in.

"His jump shot was so new . . . and he had a two-hand release from behind his head, a hesitation move, a shot that he would make no matter who was guarding him."

Fulks viewed all the publicity and acclaim realistically. "They give me the ball and I shoot," he said. "That's all there is to it."

### SAM JONES
(Boston Celtics 1957-58 through 1969-70)
- Often called the "Indispensable Celtic"
- Named to five All-Star teams
- Played on ten championship teams and scored 2,909 points in 154 playoff games
- Enjoyed his best scoring season in 1964-65 when

he shattered Tom Heinsohn's single-season record of 1,743 points, by reaching 2,070

Sam Jones' trademark was his bank shot from the corner, or anywhere around the key, which hit the backboard and angled neatly into the basket. Jones would use the backboard on most of his medium-range baskets, although the fashion of the pros in those days was to aim the shot just over the front of the rim.

"I developed the bank shot in high school because I couldn't make a layup," the 6-4 Jones recalled. "I used to spend hours by myself aiming at the strips on the backboard."

Like many superior athletes, Jones also had the remarkable talent of being in the right place at the right time. On many occasions, teammate Bill Russell would grab an offensive rebound, turn and pitch out to Jones who was standing alone, fifteen feet from the basket.

"You have to keep running and keep moving," Jones said, "and you're going to get your shots. You can't stand still. When the ball is shot, the defensive man has to turn his head to see where the rebound is going. When I see we have the rebound, I would go to another position. The man guarding me had his back to me and he never knew I moved. He had to turn around and look for me, and that's all I needed, only one second to get the shot off."

Jones was one of the great pressure players. He always seemed to play better when it mattered. Almost every year, he would average more points during the playoffs than the regular season.

*    *    *

## GEORGE MIKAN
**(Minneapolis Lakers 1948-49 through 1955-56)**

- The first of pro basketball's big men
- Won three straight scoring championships starting with the 1948-49 season
- The N.B.A.'s top rebounder, 1952-53
- Played on four All-Star teams and was the 1952-53 M.V.P.
- Scored 61 points in a playoff game against the Rochester Royals
- Led the Minneapolis Lakers to five championships
- First commissioner of the American Basketball Association

Pro basketball in the days of the 6-10, 250-pound George Mikan was more a contact and muscle game than it is today, because the center lane was only six feet wide and there was no 24-second clock. Thus the Minneapolis Lakers were able to exploit their size and style.

Mikan was just too big, strong, and talented for the players of his generation. John Kundla, the Laker coach, built his team to the standard of Mikan's strength. He gave Mikan two good rebounders in Vern Mikkelsen and Jim Polland. The ball went out to Slater Martin, Whitey Skogg, or Bob Harrison. Once the ball was cleared into the front court, the guards held up until Mikan came plodding down to take his position in the pivot. The Lakers would then throw the ball in to him and Mikan would wheel into the basket, using his elbow to mow down any opponent unfamiliar with his style. If they ganged up on Mikan, he would whip in a bounced pass to a cutting teammate that simply could not be stopped.

Mikan was named the outstanding basketball player in the first fifty years of this century. He had a tremendous effect in the game and was responsible for the rule change that widened the lane—from eight to twelve to sixteen feet.

### BOB PETTIT

(Played for the Hawk franchises in Milwaukee and St. Louis from 1953-54 through 1964-65)

- Rookie of the year 1954-55
- Never finished lower than fourth in scoring in any one season
- Won scoring titles in 1955-56 and 1958-59
- Twice named the league's Most Valuable Player
- First player to reach 20,000-point scoring plateau
- Played in eleven All-Star games and was the M.V.P. four times
- Scored a career total of 20,880 points, an average of 26.4 a game

Some years ago, during an All-Star game, Bob Pettit went up for a rebound and grabbed it away from a mad clutch of hands. But as his feet regained the floor he winced in pain. His knees crumbling, he went down hard, one hand still holding the ball, the other reaching for his leg. Ben Kerner, the team owner, leaped from his courtside seat. The look of anguish on his face was a match for the pain in Pettit's. "My team lay there on the floor, my whole franchise," said Kerner later. But only seconds went by before Pettit rose slowly to his feet. The next thing he did was to reassure

Kerner with a smile. "I'm all right," he said, "just a twinge."

The 6-9 Pettit was so steady, and dependable, he was sometimes overlooked, even taken for granted. But in this age of automation, he was an almost perfect machine. Pettit was not a deceptive player, but he was quick for a big man, with the tremendously valuable knack of following up his own shot at the basket. What set him apart from other big men were his rugged rebounding and his skillful shooting from in close— although he was just as accurate with his jump shot from beyond the foul line, or on a driving layup. Bob Pettit, in short, could do just about everything.

### BILL RUSSELL
(Boston Celtics 1956-57 through 1968-69)
- Played on eleven championship teams, including eight in a row
- Was the league's Most Valuable Player five times
- Selected to twelve All-Star teams and was the 1962-63 game's M.V.P.
- Second leading career rebounder (21,620, a game average of 22.5)
- First black coach of a major-league sports team
- Member of the Naismith Basketball Hall of Fame

A two-time All-American at the University of San Francisco and a member of the 1956 United States Olympic Team, the 6-10 Russell changed the entire concept of the game of basketball. No individual has had more influence on the trend of play in basketball since Hank Luisetti made his one-handed shot famous. Luisetti revolutionized the offense, and Russell did everything possible to cut down his opponent's point production. Russell was one of the all-time great competitors. His fierce desire for victory was insatiable. He was certainly the foremost defensive player of his day. He was quite possibly the finest defensive performer ever to play the game.

Red Auerbach has called Russell, "the single most devastating force in the history of the game. No one will ever see a defensive player of his caliber in pro basketball."

Bill Russell coached the Boston Celtics for three seasons (1966-67 through 1968-69). Then he went west and became the coach and general manager of the Seattle SuperSonics, starting with the 1973-74 season.

### DOLPH SCHAYES

(Syracuse Nationals 1948-49 through 1963-64)

- His 16 seasons stood as the all-time longevity record
- Rookie of the Year, 1948-49
- Played in 11 All-Star games
- Scored 19,249 points, ninth best on the career scoring list
- Member of the 1954-55 championship Syracuse Nationals
- Led N.B.A. in rebounding, 1950-51, and finished with a total of 11,256.
- Coached Philadelphia 76ers from 1963-64 through 1965-66 and the Buffalo Braves during the 1970-71 season.
- Member of the Naismith Hall of Fame.

Schayes played at 6-8, 220 pounds, but unlike the other big men in the N.B.A., he was not a center. Like Bob Pettit of the St. Louis Hawks, he was a corner man. Schayes had tremendous agility for his size. He was all over the court with a variety of shots. He was one of the last two-hand set shooters and could score from the outside as easily as he could drive in for a layup.

Dolph was also known as a hatchet man. Which is to say that he could use his muscles most effectively to perform his own scoring feats and to prevent opponents from performing theirs. A tireless performer, Schayes was never afraid to become involved in the rough play under the boards. When he retired he led the league in fouls committed (3,667) and free throws made (6,979).

Schayes personified the spirit of the Syracuse Nationals. Every time he would score a basket, he'd run to the opposite end of the floor and clench his fist triumphantly above his head. Though the Nats won only one N.B.A. title during Schayes' career, they never missed the playoffs.

While Schayes was at his peak, Dan Biasone, the Syracuse president, said, "We'll never truly appreciate Schayes until after his playing days are over."

### BILL SHARMAN

(Washington Capitols 1950-51; Boston Celtics 1951-52 through 1961-62)

- Member of the Naismith Basketball Hall of Fame
- Held N.B.A. record of 56 free throws until broken during 1975-76 season by Calvin Murphy of the Houston Rockets
- Played on eight All-Star teams and was the M.V.P. of the 1954-55 game
- Played on four Celtic championship teams
- Coached the San Francisco Warriors and Los An-

geles Lakers in the N.B.A. and the Utah Stars in the A.B.A.
- Won championships in both leagues.
- Stunned crowd with a 70-foot field goal in 1956-57 All-Star game.

Sharman spent much of his athletic career in the shadows. With the Celtics he played in the backcourt with Bob Cousy—and on the same team with Bill Russell. Even when he made the All-Star team, it was almost as an afterthought.

The secret of the 6-1 Sharman's success was best described in one simple word: speed. Not only was he fast on his feet, he was also the quickest shot in the game. To appreciate his bewildering style, you had to watch the way he slid downcourt. Suddenly Bob Cousy would whip the ball all the way across court from the corner. Sharman would grab it, take two swift steps, make a lightning flip, and the Celtics suddenly had two more points. The throw from Cousy to Sharman was like a touchdown pass, only more difficult to follow. His shooting was something to watch. He would cup the ball in his right hand, suddenly balancing it on his fingertips. He also shot free throws one-handed. Holding the ball at the level of his ear, he aimed it like a rifle.

# 5

# Eddie Gottlieb—the Mogul

WHEN LEW ALCINDOR was growing up and blossoming into stardom at Power Memorial Academy in New York City, the natural impulse was to compare him with Wilt Chamberlain when he played at Overbrook High School in Philadelphia. To test their accuracy, the comparison seekers were always told, "Ask Eddie Gottlieb."

Eddie Gottlieb, the Mogul, owned and coached the Philadelphia Warriors, which won the 1946-47 Basketball Association of America championship. In those days, pro basketball had not yet made a dent in the national sports scene. The B.A.A. was only the latest in a long series of leagues that had sprung up over the years, only to struggle along with minimal impact, or fail altogether.

The B.A.A. was organized to cash in on the new

popularity of intersectional college basketball and to fill the arenas that were owned and operated by hockey people.

For the 1949-50 season, the B.A.A. merged with the older National League, which had the better players, into the N.B.A. But all feats of the B.A.A. remain part of N.B.A. history. Thus, the Philadelphia Warriors' 1947 championship is where it all began.

And in his present position as "consultant" to the N.B.A. commissioner, Eddie Gottlieb still prepares the schedule for the league, a task zany enough to drive an I.B.M. computer crazy.

But the Mogul's mental power is extraordinary. His memory is almost faultless. He remembers the scores of games, the gate receipts, the attendance, and the weather conditions. His difficulty is pinpointing the exact year.

The dictionary defines a "mogul" as an important person.

"A mogul," explains Eddie Gottlieb, as a big smile breaks across his pale, heavily lined face, "is a top banana."

Gottlieb sat at his desk in the N.B.A. offices in the Madison Square Garden complex, working on the league playoff schedule, and reflecting on that championship season.

"We finished second in the East during the regular season that year," Gottlieb recalled. "The Washington Capitals won the division title. They were 49-11, and we were 35-25, fourteen games behind.

"Chicago finished first in the West, and in the play-off system, borrowed from hockey, Chicago knocked out Washington in the first round of a best-of-seven series. I suppose that was a good break for us, since we had beaten Washington only once in six games during the regular season."

Chicago's victory qualified the Stags for the final round. Meanwhile, Philadelphia defeated the St. Louis Bombers, second in the West, two games to one, and eliminated the New York Knickerbockers, the third-place finishers in the East, in another three-game series.

The Warriors, loser to the Stags in five of the six regular season games, defeated Chicago in the Championship opener, 84-71, as Joe Fulks scored 37 points, 29 in the second half. Twenty-four hours later the Warriors won again, 85-74. With Philadelphia ahead, 2-0, the series moved to Chicago.

"We were booked to take a TWA flight from Philly to Chicago," recalled Gottlieb. "The airline was going to make an attempt to set a record speed between the cities, and they thought it would be good publicity if they could set the record with a basketball team aboard. Don't forget, that first year not every team was flying regularly to games. We were the first team that flew on a regular basis.

"We were all seated, and the plane was ready for the takeoff, when Matty Guokas said he smelled smoke. He called one of the stewardesses over, and she checked with the pilots, and they found there was a small fire. In a few minutes, they transferred us all over to another plane, and we finally got to Chicago, with no record flight attempt, but in one piece, anyway."

The Warriors won again, 75-72, but the Stags took the fourth game, 74-73, and sent the series back to

Philadelphia for a fifth game. On April 22, 1947, before an overflow crowd of 8,221, the Warriors won the title, 83-80. Fulks was the high scorer with 34 points, but Howie Dallmar broke the 80-80 tie when he scored a basket with one minute of play remaining.

The Warriors began the 1946-47 season with only five or six players with pro experience. Four of them had played for Gottlieb and the South Philadelphia Hebrew Association (SPHAS), a team he had coached for many seasons in the American Basketball League.

The key to the Warriors was Joe Fulks, the league's first scoring champion and one of the top players for eight seasons. Known as "Jumpin Joe" during his collegiate days at Murray State (Ky.), Fulks was to pro basketball what Hank Luisetti was to the college game.

Playing for Stanford University, Luisetti had introduced the one-hand jump shot in 1936 against Long Island University at Madison Square Garden. His style of shooting a basketball remains with us today. Luisetti was the trailblazer. From him all else flowed, at least indirectly.

"Petey Rosenberg, who played for me with the SPHAS, told me about Fulks," said Gottlieb. "Petey had played with Fulks in the Philippines while they were in the Marine Corps during World War II. He said that if I could sign him the SPHAS would win the championship."

While Gottlieb tried to contact Fulks, the B.A.A. was formed in May of 1946 with a $50,000 salary limit set for each team. Gottlieb, who owned the Philadelphia franchise, offered Fulks the then huge sum of $5,000. Gottlieb had arrived at the salary formula by dividing the ten-player roster he had planned into the $50,000 limit.

"In my mind I thought I offered this hillbilly too much," said Gottlieb. "Then I found out who really *was* the hillbilly, because he said he would come for eight thousand dollars. I told him that was a hell of a lot of money."

Fulks eventually signed for the $8,000 he had asked for, even though Gottlieb had not even seen him play.

"I found out the first day in practice how good he was," said the Mogul. "He's the only player I know who insisted on having his own ball. No one could touch it. He shot for hours.

"In Fulks' case it wasn't just his scoring. He had that flair that only a few athletes possess—an ability to excite the crowd just by loping on the court and taking a few practice shots. Before the season was over, Fulks put so many people in the eight-thousand-arena, we bought him a five-thousand-dollar automobile as a bonus."

Fully as superstitious as any other athlete, the 6-5, 190-pound Fulks always put his right shoe on first when dressing for a game. He never passed a ball inside the locker room, and always made sure that his last shot in the pregame warmup went through the hoop.

Joe led the league in scoring in 1947 with a 23.2 average. Prior to his rookie season performance, a 14- or 15-point average by a player was considered an outstanding accomplishment.

The 63 points he scored on February 10, 1949 was the most in a single game by a player until Elgin Baylor of the 1959 Minneapolis Lakers scored 64 against the Boston Celtics. The unusual aspect of Fulks' performance was that it was accomplished in the days before the innovation of the 24-second clock. The tendency before the clock was for teams to hold the ball and stall.

In Fulks' eight pro seasons he scored 8,003 points, an average of 16.4 points a game.

Fulks, who retired from basketball in 1954, went to work as a recreational officer at the Kentucky State Penitentiary in Eddyville. When he was shot to death on March 21, 1976, basketball people recalled his greatness.

Red Auerbach, in 1946 the coach of the Washington Capitals, said, "He was a great, great player, one of the first guys who had a great variety of shots. He could shoot them any way, from any place. He set up defenses revolving about him."

"Fulks was the greatest shooter I've ever seen for a variety of shots," said Gottlieb. "I'm not saying he was the best shooter ever, but no one could match his assortment—driving hooks with either hand, jump shots with either hand, and an outside two-hand set when he got a little older. And no one could shoot better with people hanging on him—then or since.

"I can still see him scoring those sixty-three points against Indianapolis. I can remember calling a timeout and telling Joe, 'Hang around the basket, get as many as you can, because you may never have another chance like this.' I remember him saying, 'I only want 'em if I can earn 'em.' "

Gottlieb, more than anyone else, remembers the trials and tribulations of those early days because he was one of the league's organizers. He purchased the Philadelphia Warriors for $25,000. Ten years later, he sold the team for $850,000. The franchise was moved to San Francisco and he went along at a substantial salary to help get things underway.

The Mogul has been associated with pro basketball for almost 60 years, but ask him his age and the most he will admit to is "at least" 49. Around 1919, however, he was known to have scored 26 points in a game for the Philadelphia School of Pedagogy.

The Mogul can remember the ancient days when pro basketball was an adolescent, trying to survive its growing pains.

He remembers those days in Philadelphia where, in the grand ballroom of the Broadwood Hotel, for 65¢ (men) and 35¢ (ladies), you could "get the Saturday night habit of watching the SPHAS," with Chickie Passon scrambling or Stretch Meehan maneuvering under the basket. Eddie himself would be on the bench, resplendent in a loud, flowered tie, managing the team and counting the house. After the game Gil Fitch would climb out of his SPHAS basketball uniform, jump up on the stage, and lead his band as the dancing began.

"In those days," recalled Gottlieb, "many of the Jewish people wouldn't let their daughters go to an ordinary dance, except when the SPHAS were in action *before* the dance. And listen, they were good times for the young people. We even gave whats-her-name, Kitty Kallen, her start."

Besides owning the Philadelphia Warriors, Gottlieb managed football and baseball teams and once owned a Negro baseball franchise. He served as a commissioner of various leagues in several sports.

While promoting Negro baseball, Gottlieb seldom bothered with contracts, preferring instead to accept a man's word. He disliked negotiating and would set a fair price, strike a quick bargain, and settle the deal with a handshake.

When he brought Negro baseball to Yankee Stadium in 1939, he and Colonel Ed Barrow, president of the Yankees at the time, settled the deal in less than five minutes.

The Mogul's favorite story is about the day he promoted the first four-team doubleheader in Yankee Stadium. The Philadelphia Stars opposed the Pittsburgh Crawfords in the first game, and the Black Yankees were paired with the Chicago American Giants in the nightcap.

"It rained the whole night before the game," said Gottlieb, "and it really didn't stop until just before the first game started, but we had 25,000 there, and the concessions were just tremendous. Slim Jones was pitching for the stars and Satchel Paige for the Crawfords. The game was tied 1-1 in the tenth inning, so we called the game with the idea in mind that we would repeat the whole game a few weeks later, which we did. And, listen, we got about the same crowd, even though, just like the first time, it rained until the game started."

Gottlieb gained the expertise that enables him to prepare the almost 800-game N.B.A. schedule in the days when he was virtually the schedule-maker for every amateur and semipro team in Philadelphia and the surrounding area.

"We rip up a lot of pieces of paper before we get the schedule down pat," said Gottlieb. "The first thing we do is ask each club to forward a list of available dates at their arena. We also ask the teams to underline their preferred dates and from there we start.

"No team likes to be away from home too long a time. When we send a club on an extended road trip, the East to the West and vice versa, is when their arenas are booked for long periods of time. For example when the National Horse Show operates at Madison Square Garden for a ten-day period, or the ice show is in for a long stay.

"Sometimes my mind is so bogged down with schedules that I get the urge and get up in the middle of the night to work on them. But in the long run, when the schedule is finally ready, everybody is happy."

Gottlieb speaks about the early days of the ten-team B.A.A. as though it were yesterday. He even recalls the first day (but not the exact date—it was November 1, 1946) when play began in Toronto, Canada, with the Knicks beating the Toronto Huskies, 68-66.

Toronto tried hard to promote that first game. There were large three-column newspaper advertisements with a photo of George Nostrand, the tallest Toronto player at 6-8. "Can You Top This?" the ad asked. Any fan taller than Nostrand would be admitted to Maple Leaf Gardens free of charge. After all, the most expensive ticket for that game cost $2.50 (the least expensive was 75 cents), so it would be a big saving for any tall Canadian fan.

"There was a crowd of eight thousand," recalled Sonny Hertzberg, a Knick at the time. "It was interesting to play before those Canadian fans. The fans really didn't understand the game. To them, a jump ball was a faceoff. But they started to catch on and liked the action."

And that's how the N.B.A. began—with Eddie Gottlieb, the Mogul, Joe Fulks, and the Philadelphia Warriors.

# 6

# The Knicks' Impossible Victory

It was Friday night, April 18, 1969. Dave De-Busschere, pale and tired looking, sat by his locker in the crowded Knicks' dressing room in the Boston Garden, slowly sipping on a bottle of beer. There was none of the special exuberance or simple fooling around that sometimes takes place in a dressing room after a victory. Nor were there any of the sad faces that usually follow defeat.

The Knicks had just been eliminated in the Eastern Conference final of the National Basketball Association playoffs, four games to two, by the Boston Celtics, 106-105.

"That's right," said DeBusschere as he wiped off the beads of sweat that poured from his forehead, "there's no tomorrow. But there's a next year. We're in the process of building a dynasty."

Coming home on the plane from Boston, there was little talk about the imponderables: What would have

59

happened if Walt Frazier hadn't suffered a groin injury
. . . If Dick Barnett hadn't bruised his right knee and
lost his shooting touch . . . If Bill Russell, the Celtics'
domineering center who picked up his fifth foul with
nine minutes of play remaining had fouled out . . . If
Sam Jones hadn't been able to exploit Frazier's vulner-
ability . . . If John Havlicek hadn't hit an impossible
jump shot in the closing minutes?

Those were the ifs of the past. The Knicks were now
talking about the brightest possible future. The
Knicks were looking ahead, already planning their future challenge to the rest of the N.B.A.

"Just wait until next year," said Willis Reed, the
Knick captain, talking with the optimism that once belonged exclusively to the Brooklyn Dodger fans of old.

But the Knick thinking that night was sound and correct. For the next four seasons they took their fans
along on a magical merry-go-round. Basketball people
in the know were charmed by their artistry. Some fans
began calling the 1969-70 Knicks the greatest collective basketball team ever assembled.

The late Joe Lapchick, who had been associated
with the game for more than a half a century as a
player with the famed Original Celtics and a coach of
the Knicks and St. John's University, said at the time,
"This is the greatest basketball team I've ever seen.
You have to go back to the outstanding Boston Celtics
of about half a dozen years or more to compare them
with this Knick team. Only they had the Knicks' artistry. But for New York it's a collective team effort,
and Boston, despite all its greatness was primarily Bill
Russell, who covered up the Celtic mistakes.

"The Knicks relate to everybody's basketball. They
are the meeting point of the new and the old of the

sport. As a basketball oldtimer, I just sit at the games and want to rip the mooring of my seat at some of the plays they make.

"You really have to know and understand basketball to enjoy some of the things they are doing out there. They are not just playing one-on-one basketball. The ball handling, and the way they are always looking for the open man, are just beautiful to watch."

Stan Isaacs, then a sportswriter, caught the mood of the Knicks in his *Newsday* column, "Out of Left Field." He wrote: "For the Knicks these are the best times. "They are ecstatically delirious times that rank with the merriest of all sports carryings-on in New York. The Knicks are carving a place for themselves alongside the warmest of old favorites: the Brooklyn Dodgers of the Pee Wee Reese-Jackie Robinson days; the 1951 Giants of the Polo Grounds; the football Giants of Andy Robustelli-Charley Cornerly-Sam Huff days; the Yankees of the Ruth-Gehrig-DiMaggio era.

"Five men good and true. Their names are beginning to flow trippingly from the tongue: Barnett . . . Bradley . . . Frazier . . . Reed . . . DeBusschere."

Dave DeBusschere, who went on to become the commissioner of the American Basketball Association, was the final link in a long, painstaking rebuilding project which Eddie Donovan, the general manager, put together to bring New York its first championship. DeBusschere was obtained from the Detroit Pistons on December 19, 1968, in a trade for Walt Bellamy and Howard Komives.

DeBusschere became the Knicks' man Friday—the meat and potatoes man, part muscle, part mind, all seasoned experience. Off the boards, back on defense and driving on offense, he was the honest laborer, the workhorse who never had to be forced into doing his share.

At first glance, DeBusschere was not overly awesome for an N.B.A. forward. He was 6-6, 225 pounds—smaller than most. But watching his power collide with the other muscular bodies on the floor, all sinew and disciplined strength, no spectator could fail to be impressed.

Paul Silas, the Boston Celtics' powerful rebounder, once said of DeBusschere, "Dave's major asset is that he keeps coming back at you. You hit him hard once to block him out, he bangs right back in there again. He never gives up. Offensively, if you play him loose or take your eye off him, he'll sneak by you and get a pass for one of those short jumpers of his. If not that, he'll get into position to tap in a rebound."

"Professional ballplayers have a sense of pride," said DeBusschere. "No one likes to lose. There's the money, but there's more than money. Your heart's in the game or you're not in this game."

DeBusschere's approach to the game was a tribute to mental discipline.

When he played with the Detroit Pistons, Fred Zollner, then the club owner, once said, "Dave is successful because his brain is like a grapefruit. You have to pluck out a piece and have the rest stay together. You use that part for what you need, then put it back and take another section. He is so organized he can do it. He has everything tucked away somewhere in that brain."

When you asked basketball fans about DeBusschere's play, they would rave about Dave's rebounding, and wonder how he could endure the constant board fights with forwards bigger and stronger than he. They would also talk about his 20-foot jump shots that often excited the crowds. But the more knowledgeable fans also knew that DeBusschere was the finest defensive forward in the N.B.A.

When the crowd would chorus *"Deefense,"* they called DeBusschere's signal. The crowd was asking DeBusschere to direct the traffic, to snarl the offense, to make the rebound or block out another rebounder.

"If you're tired, you ease up on offense," Dave would say, "You never stall on defense; that's where the game is."

To best appreciate DeBusschere's play you had to take your eyes off the ball, forget that there was a basketball involved, and simply watch him move, watch him run his complex and seemingly endless patterns under the offensive boards, trying to run his man into someone else and thus leave himself open for either a pass or a shot. His constant movement without the ball helped make him one of the most completely selfless players in the game.

A good night's work for DeBusschere could well have been the fourth game of the Eastern Conference playoff against the Boston Celtics on April 21, 1969. Dave scored 23 points, grabbed 16 rebounds, blocked two shots, and threw his body all over the court.

Dave took John Havlicek in low, and muscled him inside with drives and an occasional hook shot. When he dove for a loose ball, three Celtics dove with him. A jump ball was called on the play, but not before Don Chaney requested a 20-second injury timeout to see if his back was still in working order.

That's the way it was from the 1969-70 season through 1972-73. This dazzling brand of basketball flashed around Madison Square Garden and throughout the N.B.A. night after night as the Knicks repeatedly brought huge crowds to their feet in joy. In winning 217 games during the four regular seasons, the Knicks became the new prophets of an old-time basketball religion.

But of all the Knicks' triumphs, perhaps the biggest one of all, occurred on the night of November 18, 1972, at Madison Square Garden.

The Knicks, losing by 18 points to the Milwaukee Bucks, 86-68, with five minutes and 50 seconds left to play, ran off 19 straight points and won the game 87-86 in a noisy and emotional finish before a capacity crowd.

After the game, the Knicks lingered. It took Walt Frazier longer than usual to slip into his new mink coat; longer for Dave DeBusschere to meet his wife, Geri, who waited in the empty runway; and longer for Bill Bradley, the usually quick leaver, to meet some of his friends.

The Knicks were trying to explain to an incredulous media, and themselves, exactly what had happened. They were not alone. Down the hall in the Milwaukee dressing room, the Bucks, also disbelieving, were doing the same thing.

"I'm sitting on the bench and watching," explained Jon McGlocklin, "and I kept saying: 'This is ridiculous. There is no way they can catch us. The way we're playing, there is no way.' The next thing I know, they've won."

Oscar Robertson, straightening his tie, putting on his jacket, said, "Don't ask me how or why. You saw it. We missed shots. Kareem had shots underneath. He just missed them. Our own fault. We went to Kareem.

We went to the big guy. He missed. That's the way it goes."

With 5:11 remaining, Earl Monroe ignited the Knicks' apparently damp fuse with a layup on a break. That shot started the Knicks on the victorious way back.

Monroe and Frazier combined for 9 straight points and then DeBusschere interrupted the backcourt men's scoring domination with a long jump shot from the left side. The rest of the scoring was left to Monroe and Frazier.

A pop from the right of the key by Monroe, and two free throws by Frazier with 47 seconds to play, drew the Knicks to within, 86-85.

Lucius Allen of the Bucks missed two free throws and Willis Reed collected the rebound. When the ball reached the other end of the court, Monroe was up to the pressure. He pumped in a 15-footer from the left side to send the Knicks into the lead.

Then Abdul-Jabbar, the game's high scorer with 32 points, was under pressure from Reed and missed for the fifth straight time, as DeBusschere grabbed the rebound.

There were 26 seconds remaining when the Knicks took possession and went into the act of trying to run out the block. Bradley, who admitted that he had two shots he might have taken, finally was called, with two seconds left, for a violation of the 24-second shooting rule.

"I just didn't realize there was extra time," Bradley said. "I guess it was because of all the excitement."

But Bradley escaped the goat's horns when Abdul-Jabbar's last-second shot fell short.

Before their comeback the Knicks were completely outplayed. Jerry Lucas was injured and didn't play. Reed, sidelined for most of the 1971-72 season, was stronger and more forceful, but still struggling with his offense. The shooting was poor. Frazier and Monroe had scored 11 points each, Bradley 14 and DeBusschere 12.

On the other hand, the Bucks were playing just great. Robertson was in complete command of the offense. Milwaukee's defenses pressured the Knicks into passing and shooting deficiencies. Milwaukee switched, jumped at the open man. Abdul-Jabbar pinned forwards in the corner, then dropped off to clog the middle.

"Our defense was great," said Larry Costello, the Bucks' coach, "Great for forty-two minutes. Then suddenly nothing. We did nothing against their fast breaks."

The breaks were part of it, but so was the Knicks' pressing man-to-man defense that Coach Red Holzman had ordered. So too, was the noise of the crowd that seemed to destroy the Bucks' poise.

"I give full credit to the crowd," said Bradley. "Tonight we'll give the game ball to the crowd."

But it was Dave DeBusschere who described the triumph best when he said, "It was an incredible game."

It sure was. An incredible season too, as the Knicks won a second N.B.A. championship and were the top defensive club in the league, yielding just 98.2 points a game. It was the fourth time in five seasons that the Knicks were tops defensively in the league. No other club since 1956-57 had held their opponents under 100 points a game for an entire season.

## HOW THE KNICKS ACCOMPLISHED THE IMPOSSIBLE

The following is a play by play description of the final wild 5 minutes and 50 seconds, wherein the Knicks scored 19 straight points and defeated the Milwaukee Bucks, 87-86:

5:50—Bob Dandridge left-side jumper, 86-68. 5:35—Walt Frazier bad pass. 5:11—Earl Monroe driving basket, fouled by Lucius Allen. Monroe converts foul, 86-71. 4:52—Bad pass by Dandridge. 4:48—Frazier scores on driving layup off turnover, 86-73. 4:15—Milwaukee calls timeout. 4:12—Frazier hits corner jumper, 86-75. 3:58—Oscar Robertson misses, Kareem Abdul-Jabbar misses follow. 3:37—Monroe scores on baseline drive, 86-77. 3:33—Robertson fumbles, Frazier recovers. 3:13—Monroe hits from outside over Chuck Terry, 86-79. 2:57—Dave DeBusschere clears board after Abdul-Jabbar misses hook shot. 2:38—Monroe misses, DeBusschere misses follow; jump ball. 2:23—DeBusschere hits after Frazier gets tap from Terry, 86-81. 2:20—Milwaukee timeout. 2:03—Dandridge misses, gets rebound, and misses. 1:49—Monroe scores on breaking layup, 86-83. 1:30—Abdul-Jabbar misses hook shot, Willis Reed grabs rebound. 1:18—Frazier misses from outside, Robertson rebounds. 0:53—Robertson misses, Bradley rebounds. 0:47—Allen fouls Frazier, Knicks call time. 0:47—Frazier makes both free throws, 86-85. Milwaukee calls time. 0:47—Robertson takes ball out at midcourt, Monroe fouls Allen for 2 shots and he misses both, Reed rebounds. 0:36—Monroe hits from key to put Knicks ahead, 87-86. 0:27—Abdul-Jabbar misses hook, DeBusschere rebounds. 0:02—Bradley holds ball as 24-second clock runs out. 0:01—Abdul-Jabbar takes pass from Allen, misses long hook along baseline, buzzer sounds, Knicks win, 87-86.

# 7

# Seeing Red

IT WAS APRIL 28, 1966, at the Boston Garden—
the night of the final game of the final series between
the Boston Celtics and the Los Angeles Lakers for the
National Basketball Association championship. For Arnold Jacob (Red) Auerbach, it was also his last game
as coach. The bristling pugnacity of his exterior personality was often so abrasive that he won no popularity contests around the league—except in Boston.

They loved Auerbach in Boston, where his coaching
genius had skillfully manipulated the Celtics from a
losing, financially troubled franchise into the most successful dynasty in all of professional sports. There was
no surer way of solidifying a hold on the affections of a
populace.

That eventful Thursday night in April, the Celtics
were going for their eighth straight N.B.A. title and
their ninth in ten seasons. Looking back, that season

appears to be pro basketball from another century and another planet.

In 1966, no one had yet dreamed up the American Basketball Association, which would start a bidding war and boost the average salary of an N.B.A. player to over $100,000. Nor had anyone even begun to dream that in only ten years the playoff pool would total $1-million, of which the winners' individual shares would be approximately $25,000.

The Celtics had finished with a 54-26 won-lost record, but the Philadelphia 76ers, with one more victory, had ended the Celtic reign of nine straight regular season Eastern Division titles. Their second-place finish forced the Celtics into a three-out-of-five game semifinal round against the Cincinnati Royals, while the 76ers drew the bye.

As the playoffs began, interest focused on whether Red Auerbach would go out a winner in his final coaching season. He had announced in January, when the Celtics were down and hurting from injuries, that this would be his last coaching season. He had been named vice president and general manager for the following season, and he is today president and general manager.

The series with the Royals permitted the Celtics to regroup their forces, to recharge their psyches. It was a tough series, unusual in that the mystique of the home-court advantage never developed. The visitors won each of the first four games, and the Celtics ended the series, 112-103, in a struggle to the end.

Next it was Philadelphia versus Boston for the Eastern Division title. The Celtics won the opener, 115-96, in Philadelphia, and the second game in Boston, 114-93. The wildest part of the second contest was a fourth-quarter fight between Billy Cunningham, the 76er rookie forward, and Larry Siegfried. During the fracas, Wilt Chamberlain, the 76er center, and Bill Russell intervened and almost came to blows themselves.

Actually, Wilt had tried to act as peacemaker by grabbing Siegfried. But Russell felt that this was not exactly a neutral method of settling the issue, and there were angry words and gestures between the two dominant giants.

Philadelphia won the third game, 111-105, Chamberlain outscoring Russell, 31-12. Still, the 76ers, leading by 24 points in the second quarter, had to fight off a consistent counter-attack, and the game was not clinched until, with 24 seconds left, Chamberlain grabbed the rebound of a John Havlicek missed shot that would have cut the lead to 2 points.

Boston won the fourth game, 114-110, as Russell outplayed Chamberlain in the second half and finally blocked a shot by Luke Jackson which would have broken a tie as regulation time ran out. In the five-minute extra session, Russell got the tap, John Havlicek scored a quick field goal, and Philadelphia never caught up. Two days later in Philadelphia, Chamberlain scored 46 points, but the Celtics won, 120-112, putting them into the final round for the tenth straight season.

The 20-year coaching career of Auerbach had dwindled down to those precious last days and the championship series against the Lakers.

Los Angeles, with a 45-35 record, had won the Western Division regular-season title, while the other four teams had played under .500 ball. The Lakers were led by Jerry West, who had finished the regular season with a 31.3 scoring average, second best to Chamberlain. They also had Elgin Baylor, who had made an amazing recovery from knee surgery but was not the Baylor of old. In the division final, the St. Louis Hawks forced the Lakers into a seven-game series before losing.

Boston roared to a 30-12 lead in the first game, and later increased its advantage to 38-20, before the Lakers tied the score in the final minute of play. The Lakers went ahead when Russell was called for goal-tending on a Baylor shot, but Sam Jones, who had missed 22 of his 29 shots during the game, scored and sent the contest into overtime. In the five-minute extra session, West and Baylor led the Lakers to a 113-129 victory.

It was an exhilarating victory for the Lakers, and a galling setback for the Celtics in Boston, but Auerbach obscured the impact the next morning when he announced that Bill Russell would succeed him as coach.

Boston won the next three games, including two in Los Angeles. The Lakers triumphed. 121-117, in the fifth game as Baylor scored 41 points, and West collected 4 points in the last 33 seconds. Back in Los Angeles, Gail Goodrich, the rookie out of U.C.L.A., collected 28 points and the Lakers evened the series, 123-115.

Now, as Auerbach made ready to coach his last and 1,585th pro game, he nervously faced his players in a locker-room pep talk. "This one means seven hundred dollars apiece to you guys. That's the difference between the winners' and losers' share. Show me another way you can make seven hundred dollars in forty-eight minutes! And remember this: If you don't win it, you'll have to spend a whole summer answering stupid questions. Ask Russ and K.C. Jones—they were on the team when we lost the title to the St. Louis Hawks in 1958. I want you to win this one for you, not for me."

If you had to single out one thing that makes Auerbach tick, it would probably be his ability to never overlook the slightest opportunity to win. Here's an example.

It was sometime in 1953. Fuzzy Levane, coach of the Milwaukee Hawks, was standing in a hotel lobby when Auerbach walked over. Red was there with the Celtics who were to be part of a N.B.A. doubleheader.

They chatted for a while and then Red whipped out the book he had just written. He took his pen and signed the book. Then he started to hand it over. But suddenly he stopped.

"Oh, no," Auerbach said to the slightly startled Levane.

"Whatsa matter, Red?" asked Fuzzy, who figured that it might have occurred to Auerbach to charge him for the book. "Let me have it," said Fuzzy. "I'd like to read it."

"I will," answered Red, "but not until after the game."

Levane laughs when he recalls the incident. "They then went out and beat us by about thirty," says Fuzz. Red Auerbach was afraid Fuzzy might learn something from the book and beat him.

Through the years, if there was a rule that had a loophole, you could depend on Auerbach to find it. No advantage was too slight, no detail was too small—if a game was on the line.

After the pregame pep talk, Auerbach gave instructions to the various players. Gail Goodrich had been driving on Bill Russell, a rare occurrence. The rookie had scored 28 points in the sixth game and Auerbach was telling his players that couldn't happen in Game 7.

"I don't want Goodrich to be an important part of the game," Auerbach told Sam Jones. "Let's concentrate on him the way we do on Baylor and West. Don't get careless with him for a minute, because the kid is a cool rookie and he can take the title away from you."

Bill Russell got the opening tap, flipped it to K.C. Jones, and he passed it off to John Havlicek cutting for the basket. Boston led 2-0 and went on to score ten straight points, six by Sam Jones. More than four minutes elapsed before the Lakers managed to score.

The Celtic defense was excellent, the fast break was working well, ignited by Russell's rebounding, and Boston led by 7 points at the quarter and 53-48, at half time.

Moments into the second half Boston's bulge reached 19, the biggest of the game, and going into the final quarter the Celtics were ahead, 76-60. With four minutes left Boston led by 13, but two baskets by Jerry West and one by Rudy LaRusso turned the home-town crowd from happy to nervous.

With 42 seconds remaining after a 35-foot jump shot by Sam Jones had been matched by a Walt Hazzard basket, Russell stuffed the ball to give the Celtics a 10-point advantage.

The crowd, sensing victory, began surrounding the court, but the celebration started too early.

Before Auerbach was to light the cigar that made all Celtic victories official—and would this year bring Boston a ninth title—the Lakers had cut the lead to 2 points with four seconds left. But the Celtics won. Although the final score was 95-93, indicating a close victory, it was actually a one-sided game. Bill Russell's 32 rebounds and 25 points were the key elements, but so were the 11 free throws the Lakers missed. Sam Jones scored 23 and Havlicek 16. West had 36 for the Lakers, but the Celtics followed Auerbach's pregame instructions. Goodrich was limited to 6 points by the tenacious guarding of Sam Jones.

Still, Auerbach didn't get a chance to puff on his victory cigar on the court. It was knocked from his mouth by the surging crowd. Minutes later, in the safety of the dressing room, he lit up another cigar and Russell, pointing to his chunky coach, said, "There is the Man. This is his team. He puts it together. He makes us win."

Before Auerbach could fight his way out of the dressing room and out of the arena, he learned that Walter Kennedy, the then N.B.A. commissioner, had fined him and Fred Schaus, the Los Angeles Laker coach, $150 each. Both coaches were also given sharp reprimands for criticizing officials in the championship playoffs.

Referee-baiting was always part of Auerbach's act. He would sometimes restrict himself, however, to a series of soulful moans or a fast flamenco step near the bench. He accumulated $1,700 in total fines at a time when penalties were far less severe than they are today. Two technical fouls are currently worth $225 and automatic expulsion from the game.

Bob Cousy can remember when Auerbach chopped up officials for breakfast, lunch, and dinner.

"In the old days, when I first came into the league," recalled Cousy, "these battles with the refs were a daily occurrence. The officials now are more competent, of course, but I think Arnold is not the firebrand he once was. But he's a real sore loser, and he expects every Celtic to be."

Auerbach has also charged into hostile crowds, as he did in St. Louis in 1962 after Sid Borgia, the chief referee, ejected him from the game. But his referee-baiting reputation, and his wars with fans, were only part of Red's general philosophy of winning.

"Sure, you go out and shake the other fellow's hand, but you would just as soon kick him in the teeth," Cousy explained. "You knew Arnold was fighting just as hard for you, making sure the refs knew they weren't going to push his team around."

Yet Auerbach never has been socially friendly with his players.

"They know I'm in their corner," Red once explained. "I'll help them in business, in private investment, or any problems they may incur, but I won't drink beer with them while they play for me."

When Cousy retired, his wife told Red at the retirement party: "You can kiss me now. Bob's not playing for you anymore." The Celtics, closer than most pro teams socially, used to invite him to parties out of courtesy, Cousy says, but they knew Red would never come.

"It's a necessary situation," Cousy declared. "You can't discipline a man if the night before you were drinking with him. A pro coach has to be more psychologist than coach. He's dealing with men who have the talent to make the best basketball league in the world. He has to use that talent to win."

As Auerbach looked wearily out of the window of his ninth-floor suite on the first morning of his retirement, he was asked whether he had been jittery while coaching his final game.

"I don't think I was." he said. "If you're jittery, your players will be jittery. Part of my life was ending, sure, but you don't approach it like a void, like a rat race into vacuum. It's not what will I do, what should I do. This is what I wanted to do."

When asked if his pep talk or his final coaching performance had anything to do with the victory, Auerbach said, "You mean, win it for me? Are you crazy? They're pros. I've never mentioned myself and I never would."

At one time, Auerbach's critics said he couldn't win without Bob Cousy. They said that Cousy ran the team. Later they would say that Frank Ramsay really coached the Celtics. The truth was that Auerbach ran the Celtics probably more than any other coach in the N.B.A.

Fred Schaus, who coached the Lakers from 1960-61 through 1966-67—and later became the Los Angeles' general manager before returning to college coaching at Purdue, once conceded:

"Auerbach is a great, great coach. A tough coach. His technical knowledge of the game is second to none. He is the only coach in the league that I worry more what he's going to do than what I'm going to do. His substitutions, his matchups, his moves are so good that you're always looking around to see what he's up to, so you can figure out how to meet it."

The Auerbach rule book called for superb conditioning, no remarks about opponents which may backfire as ammunition later, no questioning of an order, no cliques.

"One thing I've learned with the Celtics," Auerbach once said, "is to never show compassion with a winner.

I run them ragged. I never let them get over-confident."

One of his players once said, "He's the meanest, most cantankerous blankety-blank I've ever played for. But I wouldn't play for anyone else. He's a dictator, yet none of us ever suffered wrongly at his hands. Look at how many of his players are pro and college coaches."

Auerbach still contends that all pros are ex-college stars used to being pampered; so "you have to take a strong position so that they know you're the boss. Then you gently keep reminding them of it."

While Auerbach still needles the Celtics in victory, he defends them staunchly in defeat, and never has tolerated an attempt to single out a scapegoat.

Some years ago when the Cincinnati Royals, during a hot streak, challenged the Celtics for the lead, Auerbach snapped at his critics:

"Most people forget to give the opposition credit. We're not panicking."

Auerbach's attitude toward basketball has always been total commitment. He calls it the "price you pay for excellence." During his coaching days, and now as general manager, his pride in winning and sacrifice has always been part of the Celtic tradition.

## THE 20 AUERBACH SEASONS

| SEASON | TEAM | REGULAR SEASON | | PLAYOFFS | | THE OUTCOME |
|---|---|---|---|---|---|---|
| | | W | L | W | L | |
| *1946-47 | Washington | 49 | 11 | 2 | 4 | Lost to Chicago in semifinals, 2-4. |
| 1947-48 | Washington | 28 | 20 | — | — | 3-way tie for 3rd, lost to Chicago in special one-game playoff. |
| *1948-49 | Washington | 38 | 22 | 6 | 5 | Lost to Minneapolis in finals, 2-4. |
| 1949-50 | Tri-Cities | 28 | 29 | 1 | 2 | Lost to Anderson in semifinals, 1-2. |
| 1950-51 | Boston | 39 | 30 | 0 | 2 | Lost to New York in semifinals, 0-2. |
| 1951-52 | Boston | 39 | 27 | 1 | 2 | Lost to New York in semifinals, 1-2. |
| 1952-53 | Boston | 46 | 25 | 3 | 3 | Lost to New York in 2nd round, 1-3. |
| 1953-54 | Boston | 42 | 30 | 2 | 4 | Lost to Syracuse in round-robin, 0-4. |
| 1954-55 | Boston | 36 | 36 | 3 | 4 | Lost to Syracuse in 2nd round, 1-3. |
| 1955-56 | Boston | 39 | 33 | 1 | 2 | Lost to Syracuse in 1st round, 1-2. |
| *1956-57 | Boston | 44 | 28 | 7 | 3 | Beat St. Louis for title, 4-3. |
| *1957-58 | Boston | 49 | 23 | 6 | 5 | Lost to St. Louis for title, 2-4. |
| *1958-59 | Boston | 52 | 20 | 8 | 3 | Beat Minneapolis for title, 4-0. |
| *1959-60 | Boston | 59 | 16 | 8 | 5 | Beat St. Louis for title, 4-3. |
| *1960-61 | Boston | 57 | 22 | 8 | 2 | Beat St. Louis for title, 4-1. |
| *1961-62 | Boston | 60 | 20 | 8 | 6 | Beat Los Angeles for title, 4-3. |
| *1962-63 | Boston | 58 | 22 | 8 | 5 | Beat Los Angeles for title, 4-2. |
| *1963-64 | Boston | 59 | 21 | 8 | 2 | Beat San Francisco for title, 4-1. |

| | | | | | |
|---|---|---|---|---|---|
| *1964-65 | Boston | 62 | 18 | 8 | 4 | Beat Los Angeles for title, 4-1. |
| 1965-66 | Boston | 54 | 26 | 11 | 6 | Beat Los Angeles for title, 4-3. |
| | TOTALS | 938 | 479 | 99 | 69 | |

*Denotes Division championships.

# 8

# The Los Angeles Lakers' 33-Game Win Streak

AFTER THE Los Angeles Lakers had won their 27th straight game during the 1971-72 National Basketball Association season, in a streak that eventually ended at 33, it was recalled that in 1916 the New York Giants had won 26 straight baseball games. The Giants' feat had been recognized as the longest winning streak by a professional sports team.

But a letter to the *New York Times* recalled that the famous Renaissance, a touring pro basketball team, won 88 straight games during the 1932-33 season, and that the Original Celtics once had won 44 in a row. Newspaper stories reminded readers of the Passaic (N.J.) High School "Wonder Team" that won 159 consecutive games between 1915 and 1925.

Even Wilt Chamberlain got into the act and

quipped, "I played with the Globetrotters when they won 445 in a row, and they were all on the road."

The Lakers began the 1971-72 season with wandering Bill Sharman as the new coach, aging superstars Elgin Baylor, Wilt Chamberlain, and Jerry West, and a credo, "We must win everything."

Ever since Jack Kent Cooke purchased the Lakers for over $5-million from Bob Short for the 1965-66 season, he has poured millions of dollars into a new arena, hired and dismissed coaches, and juggled playing personnel.

Until the 1971-72 season, Cooke's return on his investment had been four division titles, five playoff berths, and four failures in the championship round.

The promotion of Fred Schaus from coach to general manager was the first of Cooke's major maneuvers. Then Butch van Breda Kolff was hired away from Princeton to replace Schaus as the coach for the 1967-68 season.

Cooke's next step, and perhaps the most important, came on July 9, 1968, when he obtained Wilt Chamberlain from the Philadelphia 76ers. The combination of Chamberlain, West, and Baylor immediately appeared to make the Lakers invincible—on paper. But Cooke was to learn that basketball is played with five players, not three, and championships are not won on paper.

Chamberlain, who was said to have caused several coaching changes during his career, couldn't get along with van Breda Kolff, and that led to the hiring of Joe Mullaney, a tactician from Providence College. Mullaney lasted two seasons before he was abruptly fired.

Two words can best describe Sharman's playing and coaching career: organization and dedication.

"I have never known a man like Bill," said Fred Schaus at the time. "I have done a lot of coaching in my day, but there is nothing to compare with his dedication and drive. He never stops thinking and talking basketball.

"He is continuously scribbling notes to himself. We were playing tennis a few weeks ago and he threw the ball up and was about to serve when he suddenly dropped the racquet, pulled a small pad from his pocket and wrote himself a note.

" 'I just thought of something that may give us an edge in the playoffs against the Bucks,' Sharman told me. Bill lives basketball twenty-four hours a day during the season and coaches as hard as he used to play for the Boston Celtics.

"But he's not only that way in basketball, he's like that in everything he does. Bill plays tennis just as hard, and not for relaxation but to win. I have played with and against him."

Sharman lacked the charisma of a Red Auerbach, but Sharman got his points across in the same convincing manner.

K. C. Jones, Sharman's teammate for four seasons with the Boston Celtics, described Bill as a determined player when he and Bob Cousy teamed in the backcourt.

"Sharman was just as intense during a scrimmage as he was in a game," said Jones. "I recall a scrimmage when Bill and Cousy played on the first team and Sam Jones and myself were in the opposing backcourt. Sharman went up for a shot and I blocked it. He must have taken the blocked shot as a personal insult because the next time he drove at me and scared me half to death.

"Basically, Auerbach and Sharman approach the game in similar manners. But with Red it had to be his way only; Bill seeks advice. Also, Bill is probably one of the quietest coaches in the league. While Red had a history of battling with officials and collecting technical fouls, Bill receives very few. He usually sits and watches the game intensely."

When Sharman was named the Los Angeles coach, there were whispers that he was tougher than any coach the Lakers had ever known. Sharman's reputation immediately created speculation as to how he would get along with a veteran team built on superstars who were set in their ways.

There had been stories around that one of the major reasons Rick Barry, who had played for Sharman in 1967, made his celebrated jump from the San Francisco Warriors of the N.B.A. to the new Oakland Oaks of the upstart American Basketball Association was to get away from his coach.

"He is," said Barry at the time, "a fine person, a straight person, a gentleman. But he's a miserable man to play under. He is fanatical about basketball. He eats, sleeps, and drinks the games.

"We were not permitted to talk anything but basketball, the game at hand, in the dressing room. We were not supposed to read anything besides basketball box scores. There was no world beyond the basketball court, the dressing room, or the meeting room."

In putting the Los Angeles house in order, Sharman retained his reputation as the "quiet dictator." But his actions caught the Lakers' fancy, and Wilt Chamberlain may have struck the keynote at the time when he said he had never been happier.

"Before the season started," said Sharman, "I sat

down with each player separately and told them that if there were problems concerning the way I coached, I wanted to know about it before the news media got it."

Before the start of the 1971-72 season, the predictions were for the Seattle SuperSonics to challenge for the Pacific Division title because the Lakers seemed to be worn by age and injuries. But as the Lakers won 39 of their first 42 games, it became evident that Sharman had been able to get the Lakers to play together as a team the way the Boston Celtics did when he was in their backcourt.

There was even a "new-new" Chamberlain, one who had finally learned the style of Bill Russell, his old rival. Jerry West, slowed down by injuries the season before, proved he was not over the hill. He teamed well in the backcourt with Gail Goodrich, who had returned to Los Angeles for the 1970-71 season after having spent one year with the Phoenix Suns. Finally, Elgin Baylor's retirement gave Jim McMillian the playing time he needed.

And while the Lakers were rewritting the N.B.A. record book, Sharman was saying, "I know it sounds corny, but this team is winning because of enthusiasm, pride, and dedication to hard work. Also, this is one of the most intelligent group of players I've ever been associated with."

In addition to the record 33-game winning streak, the Lakers established seven other regular-season team records, and Chamberlain and West took three of the five major individual statistical championships.

By defeating the Seattle SuperSonics on the final night of the season, Los Angeles brought its won-lost record to 69-13, surpassing the 68 victories by the 1966-67 Philadelphia 76ers. The Lakers also bettered

Philadelphia's .841 winning percentage, and the Milwaukee Buck marks of 36 victories at home and 31 on the road.

On March 19, 1972, the Lakers won a game by the largest margin in N.B.A. history—63 points—by defeating the Golden State Warriors, who had the fifth best record in the league, 162-99. Seven days later Los Angeles defeated Seattle, 124-98, to score 100 or more points for the 81st time in 82 games. This surpassed the 80 games of 100 or more points by Philadelphia, New York, and San Francisco in 1966-67, and Baltimore and Boston the following season.

Individually, Chamberlain, with a 19.2 rebounding average, won his tenth rebounding title, and with a .649 was the field-goal percentage leader for the eighth time. During that season, too, Chamberlain reached the 30,000-point milestone, and passed Bill Russell, the previous career leader in rebounds.

West, the All-Star Games's most valuable player, also won his first assist title (747) as he finished his final four games with 11, 12, 10, and 11.

In Chamberlain's prior 12 N.B.A. seasons, he had done many things. He had scored 100 points in one game, become the highest career scorer in the league, won the individual scoring championship with a 50.3 average, and acquired the assist title and nine rebounding titles. He had played the high and low posts. He was the only player to rank in the career top 10 in three statistical categories—scoring, rebounding, and assists.

The new Chamberlain finished the 1971-72 season with a 14.8 scoring average, by far the lowest of his career. Instead of scoring, he rebounded, blocked shots, and was the hub of the offense. Once he released the ball, he rarely got to touch it again. On the fast break he often remained standing in the defensive area. Even when the Lakers got into their patterns, Chamberlain handled the ball far less than he had in many years.

When the Laker offense called for throwing the ball into the post, Chamberlain would wave it around and then throw it back outside to West or Goodrich for the jump shot.

On May 7, 1972, the goal of "win everything" was realized. The Lakers defeated the New York Knickerbockers, 114-110, to clinch the best-of-seven-game championship series, 4-1. The title was the first since the franchise moved from Minneapolis to Los Angeles for the 1960-61 season.

The Lakers began their streak on November 5, 1971 with a 110-106 victory over the Baltimore Bullets, and before they were to lose again to the Milwaukee Bucks on January 9, 1972, they had beaten every club in the league at least once with the exception of the Cincinnati Royals. Los Angeles did not play the Royals until three days after the streak ended.

Almost all of the Laker victories during the streak were one-sided. One notable exception was the December 10 meeting against the Phoenix Suns.

In beating Phoenix, 126-117, in overtime, the Lakers snapped the Suns' eight-game winning streak. Goodrich scored 7 of his 32 points in the five-minute overtime on three jumpers from the 25-foot range.

The Suns made up a 14-point deficit in the final quarter when Los Angeles failed to score a basket in the last 4 minutes and 44 seconds of play. And it was Mel Counts, a former Laker, who tied the game in regulation at 111-111 with 21 seconds left to play.

Praise and champagne flowed freely after the Lakers had surpassed the Milwaukee Buck mark and beaten the Atlanta Hawks, 104-95, for their 21st successive victory.

"This team runs like Boston did a few years ago," said Sharman after the Hawks were beaten in Los Angeles. "Each man knows what his job is and he does it, but more than that, we know we can beat anybody."

During the celebration, the Lakers admitted that Sharman's preseason schedule was rigorous, with two workouts a day not uncommon, but the extra conditioning may have provided the last-minute spark that gave them their 21st victory.

The Hawks had closed to within a point with one minute to play. Then in came Gail Goodrich, who had been given a fourth-period breather, and his pass to Wilt Chamberlain under the bucket led to a dunk shot and a three-point lead with 39 seconds left.

"Yes, I definitely think we have won many games during the streak on our conditioning," said Sharman at the time. "They've worked hard and now it's paying off."

Gail Goodrich added, "It's like we put a large sum of money in the bank when the season started. Now all we're doing is drawing out the interest."

The January 9 meeting between the Lakers and the Bucks, the defending champion, in Milwaukee and on national television, was tagged the "dream game." The matchups of Wilt Chamberlain against Kareem Abdul-Jabbar and Oscar Robertson against Jerry West, paired some of the finest players in the game.

Larry Costello, the Milwaukee coach, had watched the night before when the Lakers battered the Hawks, 134-90, in Atlanta, for their 33rd victory. Costello had not seen the Lakers play since November 21 when they had beaten the Bucks, 112-105, in a game that was contested with all the fervor of a playoff game.

Despite a 39-point performance by Abdul-Jabbar, the Lakers made a definitive spurt in the final quarter and ran their winning streak to 11 in a row, equaling the club record.

Although Abdul-Jabbar had intimidated Chamberlain with his quick moves and sweeping hooks, he also turned the ball over 13 times, several at crucial junctures in the fourth quarter.

Now it was Chamberlain at 35 and Abdul-Jabbar at 25 going against each other again. They were centers of a different breed. Wilt was a defensive star rebounder and occasional scorer, and Abdul-Jabbar, then only in his third pro season, was quicker, more stylish, not as strong as Chamberlain, but more fluid, graceful, and a better scorer and foul shooter.

The Laker winning streak never had a chance. The defensive brilliance of Abdul-Jabbar, plus an impromptu "get-back" defense devised by Coach Larry Costello, gave the Bucks a 120-104 triumph.

Los Angeles led, 28-27, at the quarter and then fell steadily behind, the deficit reaching 9 points, 84-75, in the final seconds of the third period. The 7-feet-2-inch Abdul-Jabbar scored 39 points on a variety of shots and ignited a decisive 18-2 burst midway in the final quarter with a pair of baskets that ended all Laker hope.

"After scouting the Lakers in Atlanta Friday night," said Lucius Allen, the Buck backcourt man, "Larry came back with the get-back defense to cut off their fast break. We only used Kareem and one forward to rebound offensively. We kept the other forward at the foul line to prevent them from beating us downcourt."

Jerry West, who led the Laker scorers with 20 points, said, "You have to give them credit for a fine defense. I don't think we hit one breakaway basket, unless it was a twenty-foot jump shot."

Most of the Lakers and Bucks also credited Abdul-Jabbar for a fine rebounding effort that at least neutralized the board strength of Wilt Chamberlain. Abdul-Jabbar pulled down 20 rebounds, 8 more than Chamberlain. Happy Hairston led the Laker rebounders with 18.

"We knew the streak had to end sometime," said Bill Sharman. "It was one of our weakest games in quite a while, but I think we learned from it. It's hard to learn when you win."

When Jerry West was asked if he felt relieved that the streak had ended, he replied, "No, it was really a lot of fun. You just don't like to see it end this way, when we played so poorly."

Jim McMillian has since gone over to play with the Buffalo Braves, but on that Sunday, January 9, 1972, he said, "We've just finished a streak that I don't believe any other team is going to break."

### HOW THE LAKERS DID IT

| | | |
|---|---|---|
| Nov. 5 | — L.A. 110 | Baltimore 106 |
| Nov. 6 | — L.A. 105 | Golden State 89 |
| Nov. 7 | — L.A. 103 | New York 96 |
| Nov. 9 | — L.A. 122 | Chicago 109 |
| Nov. 10 | — L.A. 143 | Philadelphia 103 |
| Nov. 12 | — L.A. 115 | Seattle 107 |
| Nov. 13 | — L.A. 130 | Portland 108 |
| Nov. 14 | — L.A. 128 | Boston 115 |
| Nov. 16 | — L.A. 108 | Cleveland 90 |
| Nov. 19 | — L.A. 106 | Houston 99 |

| | | | |
|---|---|---|---|
| Nov. 21 — L.A. 112 | Milwaukee 105 |
| Nov. 25 — L.A. 139 | Seattle 115 |
| Nov. 26 — L.A. 132 | Detroit 113 |
| Nov. 28 — L.A. 138 | Seattle 121 |
| Dec. 1 — L.A. 124 | Boston 111 |
| Dec. 3 — L.A. 131 | Philadelphia 116 |
| Dec. 5 — L.A. 123 | Portland 107 |
| Dec. 8 — L.A. 125 | Houston 120 |
| Dec. 9 — L.A. 124 | Golden State 111 |
| Dec. 10 — L.A. 126 | Phoenix 117 (overtime) |
| Dec. 12 — L.A. 104 | Atlanta 95 |
| Dec. 14 — L.A. 129 | Portland 114 |
| Dec. 17 — L.A. 129 | Golden State 99 |
| Dec. 18 — L.A. 132 | Phoenix 106 |
| Dec. 19 — L.A. 154 | Philadelphia 132 |
| Dec. 21 — L.A. 117 | Buffalo 103 |
| Dec. 22 — L.A. 127 | Baltimore 120 |
| Dec. 26 — L.A. 137 | Houston 115 |
| Dec. 28 — L.A. 105 | Buffalo 87 |
| Dec. 30 — L.A. 122 | Seattle 106 |
| Jan. 2 — L.A. 122 | Boston 113 |
| Jan. 5 — L.A. 113 | Cleveland 103 |
| Jan. 7 — L.A. 134 | Atlanta 90 |

# 9

# The Battle of the Giants

ON SATURDAY, NOV. 7, 1959, Syracuse University was a 6-point favorite over Penn State in the day's top football game. Sam Snead's key putt had helped the United States take a Ryder Cup lead over England— and the National Basketball Association was struggling for acceptance.

It rained hard in Boston all day, but there would be a good gate that night for the Boston Garden game between the Celtics and the Philadelphia Warriors. The game had been sold out many weeks before. It would be the first meeting between Bill Russell and Wilt Chamberlain. The few tickets that were available from scalpers were going for $15 each, a lot of money for a pro basketball game in those days.

Russell had joined Boston two years earlier to start the Celtics on the road to a dynasty unparalleled in sports history. Chamberlain was the Warrior's 21-year-old rookie.

Russell had come into the N.B.A. after leading the University of San Francisco to two successive N.C.A.A. championships and the United States to the 1956 Olympic gold medal. Chamberlain arrived on the pro scene with luxury items most athletes of those days could not afford in a lifetime. After Chamberlain left Kansas University at the end of his junior year he had earned an estimated $75,000 playing for the Harlem Globetrotters. He owned a 13-room house, a white Cadillac convertible, and a 3-year-old colt named Spookey Cadet.

Teams usually arrive for a game about an hour and a half before the start to allow for taping, last-minute instructions, and warmup drills. As the Warriors and Celtics arrived at the Boston Garden, few empty seats remained.

When the teams finally came out for their warmups, the crowd surrounded the floor at both ends of the court. There they watched Chamberlain, all 85 inches of him, take his awesome, patented dunk shots and Russel sink his less spectacular push and hook shots.

Aware this was one of the great moments in sports, the two centers—Russell, who was to carry the tag of Mr. Defense, and Chamberlain, who was to become the most devastating offensive force associated with the game—stopped shooting and met briefly at center court. Chamberlain, joking and at ease, quickly destroyed the image of nervous-rookie-about-to-do-battle-with-established star. Russell, however. was serious for the entire meeting.

When the game began, Russell and Chamberlain appeared to revert to type. Chamberlain tried a fallaway, one-handed jump shot and had it blocked for the first time in his career. Time after time Wilt tried the shot, but his aim was distorted by Russell's huge hands waving in his face. Discouraged, Chamberlain switched to his less effective hook shot. With Russell keeping Wilt in check, the superior Celtics raced to a 76-61 halftime advantage and remained in control the remainder of the way.

At games' end, the Celtics had triumphed, 115-106—their sixth straight victory, while the Warriors were beaten for the first time in four games. Chamberlain outscored Russell, 30-22, but he had taken twice as many shots from the floor, 39-18, and only four of his 12 baskets came on a man-to-man situation.

Russell won the rebounding battle, 35-28, and the partisan Celtic crowd gave their favorite giant a standing ovation. Minutes later, in the Celtic dressing room, a reporter told Russ, "They're cheering you, Bill." Russell responded with praise for Chamberlain and predicted that before the end of the season, Wilt would be one of the greatest players of all time.

That first meeting was the prelude to a decade of confrontations between the two friendly giants. And every time they met, another chapter was added to the ageless struggle of defense versus offense.

Chamberlain averaged 37.6 points in his rookie season, but against Bill Russell & Co. it was 39 points. Russell, however, clamped down during the playoffs and limited Wilt to a 30.5 points.

Through the years, Russell's pride had enabled him to successfully battle the taller, 280-pound Chamberlain. To stop him, Russell had to be psychologically ready. Even then, there was never a sure guarantee that he would be up to the task.

On Jan. 14, 1962, Wilt scored 62 points against Russell, a Boston Garden court record. When Wilt's game was right, there was no one with the strength to stop him. One night when he scored 49 points against Russell and so outplayed him, the Celtic star sat in the locker room and cried.

"I'm a grown man," Russell was later to recall, "and I don't cry often, but I cried that night."

But Russell had his nights against Chamberlain, a fact even Wilt once conceded.

"Russell," said Chamberlain, "is more effective against me than any defender in the N.B.A. because he catches me off-guard with his moves. Sometimes, he plays in front to deny me the ball. Other times, he's in back of me. He has me guessing by playing me tight one game and loose the next. When I look around to find out where he is, it means losing concentration on my shot. Of course no one ever had the timing to block shots the way Russ does."

On one occasion Russell held Chamberlain to 2 points and no field goals over a 20-minute span.

The 1961-62 season was one of Chamberlain's most spectacular. In that season, he rewrote the N.B.A. record books. He scored 100 points against the New York Knicks in one game and finished the season with a 50.4 scoring average. But when playoff time came, the one-man scoring machine had his average cut down to 33.6 points against the Celtics.

The Russell-Chamberlain rivalry was good for the N.B.A. It spilled over from the basketball court to the fans, players, and coaches. It even had an effect on salary negotiations. In 1965, Russell publicly stipulated that he had signed a contract for $1 more than the $125,000 Wilt was reported to be earning.

In barrooms, playgrounds, and every other place where people talked basketball, arguments raged as to whether Wilt or Russell was the better player.

To answer that question was to unearth the age-old clichés: "Best offense is a good defense," and "You can't win without scoring."

After the 1965-66 season, Red Auerbach traded 20 seasons of coaching to become the Celtic general manager. He hand-picked Russell as his successor. In Russ' first season as player-coach, the Philadelphia 76ers interrupted Boston's eight-season reign as the N.B.A. champion.

With the 76er victory came a new Chamberlain. His season scoring average dipped to 24.1 points. Instead of leading the team in scoring, Wilt became more of a team player. He led the league in field-goal percentage (.683), rebounds (24.2), and he was third in assists (7.8).

Alex Hannum, then the Philly coach, called his team the greatest in the history of pro basketball. Hannum's remarks brought an immediate rebuttal from the Celtics.

"I wouldn't expect Hannum to say anything else," said Russell. "I'd say the same thing if I was their coach. Apparently Hannum forgot all about the teams that could easily have beaten the 76ers. Our 1960-61 team, for instance, was a pretty good one."

But no one denied that Chamberlain was the major cog in the championship-season wheel, not even Red Auerbach—never one of Wilt's biggest boosters.

In Red's book, *Winning the Hard Way*, he wrote, "Chamberlain never joined the team. It was the other way around for Russell."

While Auerbach finally took time to find some kind

words for Chamberlain, Russell once explained: "Wilt's attitude has not been as good as people have thought. When Chamberlain first came into the league he had a different concept of the game than I had. Now his play is the same as mine. He has been playing the way I played for the last ten seasons. He did it better than I used to do it, but it's the same game—passing off, coming out to set up screens, picking up guys outside and sacrificing for team play."

The 76ers of 1967-68 were heavily favored to repeat. With their youth and power, they were to be the coming dynasty, while the Celtics, an old empire, were supposed to have passed their glory days.

It didn't happen that way. There was a lot left in Bill Russell. The Celtics came roaring back and eliminated Philadelphia in the Eastern Conference playoff final, four games to three.

After the game that sent the Celtics into the championship round against the Los Angeles Lakers, Larry Merchant wrote in the *New York Post*:

"And Chamberlain, with dramatic correctness, stood out in the final for not standing out. He scored only 14 points—and took just one shot in the second half. Never mind his 34 rebounds. Never mind the crippling injuries that turned the 76ers into basket cases instead of shooters. Never mind the super defense played by an aroused Bill Russell, Wilt Chamberlain took one shot in the second half, which says it all."

Chamberlain and Russell have had varying careers on and off the court. People have tended to ask Wilt to prove and reprove his talent, although he has been the most devastating individual force in the N.B.A. Not so with Russell. He was always accepted as a team player and a winner.

Actually, Wilt was a man driven to accomplishment, a staunch believer that nothing was beyond his grasp. He met every challenge the game offered. When he was called merely a scorer, he changed his attack and became a feeder. When the second-guessers said he couldn't block shots like Russell's, he proved that he could.

Chamberlain was the first center in N.B.A. history to lead the league in assists (.702). He never fouled out of a game, and when he left the N.B.A. after 14 seasons he had scored 31,419 points, an average of 30.1 points a game.

"He can do anything in basketball," Alex Hannum, who coached Wilt both in San Francisco and Philadelphia, once said.

Yet, when Chamberlain didn't always measure up to his own high standards, he was maligned in the media and booed on the court. The paying customers felt cheated.

Russell, on the other hand, became an accepted national institution on the court, and a controversial figure off it.

During Russell's waning playing days, Cliff Keane wrote in the *Boston Globe*, "Back a few years, everyone in the league said that the day Bill Russell started to fade, forget the Celtics. They claimed they never worried about the Cousys, Heinsohns, or Sharmans. Take Russell off the court and it's good-bye."

Keane's prognosis proved correct. After Russell's retirement in 1969, the Celtics missed the playoffs for two successive seasons before Dave Cowens, the new-breed center, arrived on the scene and restored the dynasty to its former position of power.

The Boston team had gone through a great deal of

trouble to obtain Russell. With Bob Cousy, Bill Sharman and Ed Macauley, the Celtics usually led the N.B.A in scoring but never finished first. The Celtic problem was the lack of a big man. Macauley, the center, was too frail to withstand the physical contact in the battle of the boards.

To obtain Russell the Celtics had to give up Macauley and Cliff Hagan, the highly touted rookie, to the Hawks in exchange for St. Louis' first-round draft choice. The Hawks had the second pick in the draft behind the Rochester Royals.

The Royals presented no problem in the acquisition of Russell. Rochester had assured Walter Brown, the then Celtic owner, that they would choose Sihugo Green in the draft. The only problem Boston now faced was signing Russell. They had to wait for Russell's return from playing with the U.S. Olympic team in Australia.

When Russell finally became a Celtic, he gave Boston some anxious moments as to whether they had made the correct move. Russ had to learn a new system of basketball. In college he had played a disciplined ball-control offense. The strategy was to work the ball into Russell close to the basket.

The Celtics thrived on the fast break. That called for Russell to dominate the defensive boards and get the ball out quickly, while the rest of the team broke downcourt. It was the Celtic strategy then, it remains their strategy today.

In addition to the new-style offense, Russell had to adjust to the rough board-play. The first time he came into Madison Square Garden to play against the Knicks, Harry Gallatin gave him his first major lesson in the battle of the boards, where elbows fly. Gallatin completely outplayed Russell by moving away from the basket to obtain more shooting room over the Celtic center. The Knick strategy took away much of Russell's advantage as a rebounder.

After the game, Russell was to say, "My education will go on for some time. Until I die. I hope when I stop learning I'll quit."

That has always been Russ' credo.

# 10

# The Fabulous Fifth—
# The Triple-Overtime Thriller

THIRTEEN NATIONAL Basketball Association banners hang from the rafters of the old Boston Garden. Each was put there by a Boston Celtic championship, filled with sentiment and memories of great basketball moments. But as long as people compare and discuss sports, arguments will always develop over whether the fifth game of the championship series between the Boston Celtics and the Phoenix Suns, on June 4, 1976, was the best and most exciting basketball game ever played.

The following day, newspapers throughout the nation proclaimed the game "The Fabulous Fifth." Some called it the greatest game ever played. But in news stories, columns, and editorials all agreed that it was a game against which all future aspirants to greatness will be measured. It was a game not only notable for extraordinarily spectacular plays, but for the amount of human frailty embodied therein.

Soon after the Celtics had beaten the Suns, 128-126, in the first triple-overtime game in the history of the N.B.A. finals, Tom Heinsohn, the Boston coach, who stands 6 feet 7 inches and weighs in somewhere around the 300-pound mark, had to be assisted to the trainer's room. Once there, he blacked out—suffering from nervous exhaustion.

Meanwhile, in the Phoenix dressing room, Ricky Sobers, the pugnacious rookie guard, sat with his head in his hands, complaining of feeling weak and dizzy. And down the hall, in the Celtic dressing room, Paul Silas, the bedrock of the Celtics, looked wearily at his tattered sneakers and wondered out loud: "Can these go one more game? Can I?"

It took 63 minutes of playing time, spread over three hours and eight minutes of debris-throwing and name-calling, for the Celtics to take a 3-2 edge in the best-of-seven-game series. Before the game was over, hundreds of young people in the capacity crowd of 15,320 at the Boston Garden tried to swarm to the players. Many in the crowd were hauled away by police for fighting with the referees, the players, the coaches, the broadcasters, the ushers, and each other.

Rick Barry of the Golden State Warriors, serving as an analyst for CBS during the series, had a soda thrown at him. A member of the crew of a local television station had to be treated for a leg injury after the game. Richie Powers, one of the officials, could not quite make it to the safety of the dressing room. As thousands stormed the court, Powers was confronted by a fan. Powers first raised his hands to defend himself, then switched to throwing punches.

Two days later the Celtics defeated the Suns, 87-80, for their 13th championship in 20 seasons.

Never did the Celtics appear invincible. At times their offense sputtered as they went four, five, and even eight minutes without scoring a basket. Rarely did they flash the old-style fast break of Celtic renown. Instead, they were a team that played well when they had to and found a new hero when they had to. What kept them alive in many games was honest defense, intelligence, and hard manual labor under the boards by Dave Cowens and Paul Silas, better known as the greatest one-two muscle duo in basketball.

Red Auerbach said of the 1976-77 Celtics, "This team had to scratch and claw for everything. Never once in these playoffs did I chew them out. You know, give them the zing like I did in other years. They did the best they could."

What the best amounted to was in the Celtic tradition. The names on the team changed from Bill Russell and Bob Cousy to Dave Cowens, Jo Jo White, and Charlie Scott, but the character of the team remained the same.

John Havlicek once explained the Celtic tradition best when he said, "The rookies, the young players, they learn through osmosis. They look and they absorb. They see what it is to be part of this team. It's the long green line, and there is always someone to step in, to take over."

In 1975, it was Scott joining the company of Dave Cowens, Jo Jo White, John Havlicek, and Paul Silas. Scott was acquired from the Phoenix Suns in a trade for Paul Westphal.

It didn't take long for Scott to get a taste of Celtic tradition. After the Celtics' first home game, he said, "I looked up and saw all those championship flags on the ceiling, and the feeling just captured you. It was more like college that way, with an esprit de corps. You feel like you're part of the family."

The Boston family, of course, makes certain demands on its players. "All they asked me to do," said Scott, an elongated guard with quickness, tremendous speed, outstanding range, and an amazing wingspan, "is hustle every day, to play hard and hustle."

When the 1975 Celtic training camp opened, a rookie tried to beg off doing wind sprints.

"What's the matter?" Paul Silas asked.

"I've got cramps," the rookie explained.

"We've all got cramps," Silas snapped back.

The rookie did his wind sprints.

Boston began slowly, but when the regular season ended on April 11 in Washington, a rejuvenated John Havlicek had scored 38 points to lead the team past the Bullets, 103-99. The Celtics had won the Atlantic Division title, even though they were never really the favorite. At the start of the season, the Buffalo Braves figured to win in the Atlantic Division, Washington was supposed to be the major playoff obstacle in the East, and the Golden State Warriors were to be the final test.

Instead, the Celtics beat out Buffalo and Philadelphia by eight games each in the Atlantic Division and then eliminated Buffalo in six somewhat easy games in the playoffs. The Celtics never had to play either Washington or Golden State. The Cleveland Cavaliers had eliminated the Bullets and the Phoenix Suns had put out Golden State, the defending champion.

For the Phoenix Suns it was a fairy-tale season. In

carrying the championship series to six games, they, too, had won in a sense. The Suns, with two rookies in the starting lineup, center Alvan Adams and guard Ricky Sobers, were in last place as late as February 1. That's when they found the missing piece to their jigsaw puzzle in the form of the power forward Gar Heard, obtained in a trade with the Buffalo Braves. From then on, the Suns played steady ball and clinched a playoff berth with some big victories in the final week of the season.

Still, the Suns finished in third place in the Pacific Division, 17 games behind the Golden State Warriors, the division champion. Never before had a team so far down in the standings reached the final round. The closest such feat was performed by the 1959 Minneapolis Lakers, who finished 16 games behind the St. Louis Hawks and then made it to the final against the Boston Celtics.

After Phoenix had eliminated the Seattle SuperSonics in the first round of the Western Conference playoffs, the question most people asked was, "Who were these faceless Suns?"

Since Charlie Scott had played three seasons in Phoenix before coming to Boston, he was the authority on the Suns. To the inevitable questions, Charlie would reply, "They are a great ball-moving team. They are a team of eager kids lusting for their first test of fame."

Yet nobody gave the Suns a chance against the Warriors in the second round. But the Suns established their credibility by winning the second game in Oakland, and from then on it was the series. The key game was the fourth, a spectacular double-overtime triumph. But the game which changed the Suns' image was the seventh, played in Oakland.

Tension was high for the seventh game. Everyone was waiting for the Suns to crack. Even though they were down 10 points at one point in the second period, they did just the opposite. The Suns broke open a tight game with eight straight fourth-quarter points, and then protected their lead brilliantly to nail down their first Western Conference title, 94-86. From last place in February to a conference championship in May, was a fabulous, meteoric rise.

Now the stage was set: the amazing Phoenix Suns against the awesome Boston Celtics—the new kid on the block against the all-time king of the hill.

The Celts had beaten the Suns seven straight times over a two-season span, but that was a statistic both teams ignored. Still, the Phoenix-Boston matchup figured to be the most one-sided series in the thirty-year history of the N.B.A.

The Suns missed 62 percent of their field-goal attempts and lost, 98-97, in the opener. Then they were beaten, 105-90, in the second contest. The fans again questioned whether the Suns were just lucky to get by the Golden State Warriors and if they really belonged in the final round.

When the Celtics arrived in Phoenix for the third and fourth games, Tommy Heinsohn, the Boston coach, analyzed the situation and said, "The Suns have got their thing going for them out here—the sun, the heat, the pools, and all that jazz. It will be a big factor against us. They may have had their backs to the wall, but they'll be in front of that big home crowd."

Heinsohn was correct. Paranoia power was turned on full-blast and Phoenix won, 105-98, as Alvan Adams, the Oklahoma Kid and the rookie of the year, scored 33 points and pulled down 14 rebounds.

The Celtics trailed most of the way in game four—rallying to within two points eight different times in the fourth period, the last time with 13 seconds left, before losing, 109-107.

If game five did nothing else for N.B.A. history, it accomplished two things for sure: It elevated the 30th final playoff series from gripe to greatness, and it proved that the Suns, funny suits, Thom McAn shoes, college offense, and all, belonged.

The way the Celtics attacked in the first quarter, the bizarre ending to the "Fabulous Fifth" was hardly expected. The Suns were down, 32-12, after nine minutes, 36-18, at the quarter, and at one point Boston led by 22 points—its largest margin of the game. Havlicek, White, and Cowens had controlled the boards and helped in the 61 percent shooting first quarter. At no time during the playoffs did the Celtics play better than in those inspired 12 minutes.

But the Suns fought back, as they had done so often in their late charge to glory. They refused to fold. MacLeod had taken a diverse group of veterans—some of them castoffs—and rookies and molded a tough team. Systematically running their clockwork offense, the Suns patiently chipped away. The Celtics, forced to shoot from the outside, scored only 34 second-half points.

The Suns trailed, 61-45, at halftime. Then they hit Boston with a 19-7 surge that cut the lead to 68-64. But the Celtics recovered quickly, and when a Havlicek jump shot made it 92-83, with 3:49 left, it appeared as though the Suns were beaten. But Paul Westphal, once the Celtics' 1972 top draft choice, then began to express his vengeance for being traded. He scored nine of the next 11 Sun points, including a three-point play which tied the game at 94-all with 39 seconds left.

Seventeen seconds later the Suns' comeback seemed complete when Curtis Perry made a free-throw to put them ahead 95-94. But Alvan Adams committed his sixth personal foul, forcing him out of the game. With Havlicek at the foul line for two shots and only 19 seconds left, it appeared he was ready to ice the game for a nice, normal finish. But the Celtic captain made the first to tie the game—and missed the second.

Havlicek got the ball back again with three seconds left on the regulation clock. He shot from the corner, but the ball bounced off the rim into a Phoenix player's hands. The Suns called timeout for one more shot which Heard missed, to set the stage for the first of the three overtimes.

In the first five-minute overtime, each team scored six points. The Celtics went ahead, 101-97, on a baseline jumper by Jo Jo White with 1:58 remaining, but a turnaround 14-footer by Curtis Perry, and a 10-foot baseline fallaway with 45 seconds left, tied the score at 101-all and set up what was to be the most bizarre of the extra sessions.

Trailing, 109-106, with 19 seconds to go, Dick Van-Arsdale hit his only basket of the game. Westphal stole the ensuing inbounds pass from Havlicek and fed it to Perry, whose jumper put the Suns ahead, 110-109, with five seconds remaining.

However, Havlicek, no stranger to the task, sent the crowd into a frenzy as he made a running jumper. Everyone in the Boston Garden thought the game was over and hundreds of young people tried to get to the players. The security police had completely lost control. But wait! Richie Powers, one of the two officials, determined there still was still one second to go. The crowd was finally persuaded to return to the sidelines, chanting, "We're number one!"

The final second proved to be sufficient time to set up a third overtime. For openers, Westphal suggested that the Suns take a time out—even though none remained, and a technical foul would be called. His reasoning was even though the Celtics might go two points up, the Suns would get the ball at mid-court instead of under their own basket. Westphal's thought proved to be a touch of genius. After Jo Jo White made the technical foul that put the Celtics ahead, 112-110, Heard took an inbounds pass and made a 20-foot jumper to tie the game.

"One second is a lotta time," Heard was later to say. "I knew I could get the shot off. Don Nelson was overplaying me because he was afraid I was going to the basket."

MacLeod said, "Thank God for Westphal's timeout. At the time it saved us."

Whereas the first two overtimes had featured incredible clutch shooting by Jo Jo White of the Celtics and Ricky Sobers, Gar Heard, and Paul Westphal for Phoenix, the third overtime belonged to Glenn McDonald, the little-used sub, who came off the bench when Silas fouled out. McDonald played a superb 63 seconds, scoring two baskets and two free throws to give Boston a 126-120 advantage with 36 seconds left.

When the third overtime began, some impressive players were watching from the bench. Alvan Adams, Dave Cowens, Charlie Scott, and Paul Silas had all fouled out. Westphal tried some more heroics with two wondrous shots—a banked fallaway from 20 feet on the right side and a 360-degree spinning righthander in the lane, but he was no match for White and McDonald. The pair combined for 12 points in the last overtime and Jim Ard, Cowens' understudy, hit two free throws that proved the winning points.

No one will recall that the Suns came from 22 points down in the first quarter, when it appeared the Celtics were going to blow them right back to Phoenix. What people will best remember is that the Celtics prevailed in a classic game on the night all hell broke loose in Boston. They will also remember that the Suns could have folded up and gone home.

Instead, the Suns proved they belonged.

As McLeod fought his way through the crowd to the dressing room after the game, he said, "People thought we were a bunch of guys from the West who shouldn't have been here. What do they think now?"

# 11

# The Arrival of the
# New Kid on the Block

THE PLACE WAS Freedom Hall in Louisville, Kentucky, and a minute and a half remained in the 1969 National Collegiate Athletic Association championship game between the University of California, Los Angeles and Purdue. Lew Alcindor, 7 feet 1⅛ inches, with a standing reach of 9 feet, size 16D basketball shoes, and hands that could curl around a basketball as though it were a grapefruit, stood near the free-throw line, holding the ball over his head.

It was an almost comical Mutt and Jeff setting. Doomed to futility, Billy Keller of Purdue, 5-10, was clawing fanatically to get the ball.

When the game was over Alcindor had scored 37 points and otherwise demoralized Purdue as U.C.L.A. won its third straight championship, 88-82. The young giant was chosen the tournament's most valuable player for the third successive year.

Basketball victories and championships had become synonymous with the Alcindor name. The New York-bred superstar played in only three losing games during his last seven years of high school and college competition.

Born Ferdinand Lewis Alcindor, Jr., on April 16, 1947, he began to show interest in the Islamic faith while a history major at U.C.L.A. In 1969 he became a Muslim, but it was not until two years later, prior to making a three-week tour of African countries for the State Department, that he revealed the Islamic name he preferred to be known by: Kareem Abdul-Jabbar.

"When I'm speaking to people and holding news conferences I want to use my Islamic name," Kareem said at the time. "I hope to get respect from my countrymen. I realize that I've become a public figure with my Christian name and I don't expect the Milwaukee Bucks to change it."

A short time later, however, the Bucks complied with Kareem's wishes and in a news release announced that in the future his wishes would be followed. The new Muslim name translated into "generous," "servant of Allah," and "powerful."

Long before Kareem played his final game for U.C.L.A., the National Basketball Association had decided that his draft rights belonged to the Milwaukee Bucks. The decision was made in a heralded coin toss involving the Bucks and the Phoenix Suns—both expansion teams who had finished their seasons with the worst won-lost records in their respective conferences.

The coin toss by telephone, often called the most famous in N.B.A. history, was conducted by then commissioner Walter Kennedy from his 23rd-floor office at New York's Madison Square Garden complex.

Dick Bloch, the Suns' president, was on one end of the telephone line in Phoenix, and John Erickson, then vice-president and general manager of the Bucks, listened to the proceedings from Milwaukee.

Prior to the coin toss, the Suns had conducted a fan vote to advise Bloch on whether he should call heads or tails. The balloting favored heads.

Kennedy flipped the silver 50-cent piece into the air. Bloch called, "Heads." The coin came up tails, and in Milwaukee, Wes Pavalon, then principal owner of the Bucks, embraced John Erickson so exuberantly that he jammed his lighted cigarette into Erickson's ear.

Milwaukee had tried to support professional basketball before, in the early 1950s. The community effort failed and the Hawks moved to St. Louis, where they prospered until hockey swept down the Mississippi and forced them on to Atlanta.

Pavalon, a man of means, had organized the syndicate which brought pro basketball back to Milwaukee. Now, with the rights for Abdul-Jabber, all he had to do was sign him. The American Basketball Association had come into being in 1968, and the fledgling league had awarded the rights to Abdul-Jabbar to the New York franchise.

The Nets, at the time, were owned by Arthur J. Brown, a trucking magnet, but he failed to match the Bucks' offer and Milwaukee signed Kareem to a $1.4-million contract on April 3, 1969.

Abdul-Jabbar was not the first of pro basketball's magnificent giants. Bill Russell and Wilt Chamberlain had preceded him, but neither had stirred the nation's imagination as much as the arrival of Kareem. Russell and Chamberlain had entered the pro ranks at a time when the N.B.A. was struggling for recognition. Abdul-Jabbar's entrance came when television had virtually transformed the popularity of college and pro basketball.

In the ensuing months after the signing, the pro basketball world waited anxiously for Abdul-Jabbar's debut. During the interim, Kareem was the cover boy on one sports magazine after another. Some writers were already predicting his future greatness, comparing him with Russell and Chamberlain. One story was entitled "Superstar or Cardiff Giant?"

Unofficially, the pro basketball season is preceded by several All-Star games, the most famous of which is the Maurice Stokes Memorial, played annually at Kutsher's Country Club in Monticello, New York. Initially, the players came at their own expense from all over the country to help raise money for the support of Stokes, the former Cincinnati Royals star who was struck down by an attack of paralyzing encephalitis. Since Stokes' death, the game has continued to support needy basketball causes and helped keep Stokes' memory alive.

It was at the 11th annual game, on August 19, 1969, that Abdul-Jabbar quickly proved he would be an outstanding pro. After the game, Kareem walked away with a straight-A rating from Wilt Chamberlain, the greatest scorer in N.B.A. history.

Chamberlain and Abdul-Jabbar played on opposite All-Star teams. On the first play, the more experienced Wilt took Kareem inside and whirled in on him for a stuff shot. That set the tempo for the game as the giants led fast-break attacks for their respective teams.

The fans knew that Chamberlain was tough. What

they really wanted to know was how Kareem stacked up against the best competition.

Kareem did well. He impressed some of the greatest names in pro basketball.

"That boy is good," said Wilt. "There's no ifs, ands, or buts. His ability was no surprise to me. I've been watching him since he was a seventh grader."

Wilt was joined in his thinking by Walt Frazier and Willis Reed, who played in the game as representatives of the Knicks, and by Red Auerbach, Abdul-Jabbar's coach in that game.

"It's tough enough that he's seven feet," said Reed, who was to have several outstanding battles against Kareem, "but to be seven feet and have his quickness, wow!"

"He has some things to learn," Auerbach added. "Once he let Zelmo Beaty lock his arms and that could cost a game. But he'll pick those things up quickly. He's great, he's quick, and he knows what he's doing on the court."

And what did Kareem think of his initial encounter in the world of pro basketball?

"Well," he said, a grin breaking across his youthful face, "in the pros, it's all one-on-one. There are no zones."

Pro basketball, with all the pushing, shoving, and grueling play, had to be a relief for Kareem. Scholastic and college coaches, and their players, had tried to stop him by harassment and a number of other harrowing means.

When someone had reminded Kareem that in the pros he would get belted and bruised, he quickly retorted, "I'll have to learn to cope with it." And then with a smile he added, "In the pros, you can push back."

The Suns had lost the coin toss for Kareem, but they were smart enough to bring him to Phoenix for a preseason game. Some 10,000 people, only a few under capacity, paid to see how well Abdul-Jabbar would do—and what they had lost.

When the ball was tossed up to start the game, Kareem jumped high into the air and tapped it back to a teammate. He then went downcourt in a long, deceptive lope that placed him under the basket seconds later. After jockeying for position, he reached for a pass, dribbled and faked to his right and, with the precision of a small man, tossed a soft, short shot into the basket.

In that game, Phoenix also displayed a new and talented player, Connie Hawkins, a transplant from the American Basketball Association. But the excitement of the close contest, won by Milwaukee, 87-86, and the virtuoso performance of Hawkins were both lost in the shadow of Alcindor's brilliance. He scored 24 points, had 23 rebounds, and blocked 11 shots.

Kareem had shown the crowd that he was as close to a blend of Wilt Chamberlain and Bill Russell as a novice pro could be and remain human.

The Suns failed in their attempts for easy shots because Kareem was there to block them. Late in the game, when Phoenix threatened, he batted away a shot from 10 feet out, came back under the basket, and batted down the follow-up. Then he virtually crammed the ball down a Sun-shooter's throat when he tried to tip it in. The next time Phoenix came downcourt, Kareem again batted the ball away, recovered it, and tossed a lead pass to a teammate running the break that enabled Milwaukee to score. Offensively, he moved more quickly than Chamberlain and proved to be a better shot than Russell.

Once he took a pass at the free-throw line, faked the defender and, his long, lean body stretched taut, leaped and stuffed the ball through the basket.

Guy Rodgers, Abdul-Jabbar's teammate at the time and noted as the man who used to feed Chamberlain, said, "He's the most agile big man I ever saw, and the fastest. He moves around. You pass him the ball and he can put it down, move on the man guarding him, and score. And he's great at the lead pass to start a fast break."

The Bucks were scheduled to open their 1969-70 season against the Detroit Pistons on October 18 at Milwaukee. Since Milwaukee was in the heart of college football territory, it normally would have been just another pro basketball game.

But Kareem had changed all that. He had excited the nation and the American Broadcasting Company, which at the time held the contract to televise pro basketball. Usually, the pro basketball season did not begin on TV until January, after the close of the football season. But sensing the Abdul-Jabbar excitement, the network juggled its schedule in order to telecast the Milwaukee-Detroit opener.

ABC gave the game extra-special treatment. The network assigned an extra camera crew to concentrate on Kareem during timeouts. It also put in two extra rows of lights over the Milwaukee arena floor to bring the candle power to the required intensity for the color telecast. The equipment, brought in all the way from New York and not from nearby Chicago, filled three huge trucks that took up almost a city block.

Before the season opener, Coach Larry Costello

gave his players their final instructions. He reminded them constantly to get the ball into Kareem in the middle whenever possible. It was an offense new to the Bucks. In the previous season, Milwaukee, forced to use the aging Wayne Embry at center, relied more on the outside shooting of Jon McGlocklin and Flynn Robinson, its high-scoring backcourt.

"It's not easy to break a habit," said Costello, "but when you've got a guy like Kareem, you've got to use him. Not many centers in the league are going to stop him in one-on-one situations."

Through the years Kareem has been the subject of endless debate. Some fans contend that his greatness is due to his overpowering height. But that contention has been disputed by knowledgeable basketball people.

As spectators watched Abdul-Jabbar grow into the most dominant force in pro basketball, it was easy to forget about his height when he operated around the basket. He looks more like a smaller man when he throws his head and body fakes at opponents.

"Look at his hands, the quickness in the way he dribbles," said Wayne Embry, who later became the Bucks' general manager. "You undoubtedly heard people say he wouldn't be playing pro basketball if he were not seven feet tall. They are wrong, he would be playing in this league if he was five-eleven."

Pete Newell, once the Los Angeles Lakers' general manager, said, "Kareem's body is as well tapered as any player in the league, regardless of size. His leg development is beyond a man of his size. Bill Russell and Willis Reed had great upper-torso developments. Wilt Chamberlain is probably the strongest athlete I've seen, but none has the leg development Kareem has."

But perhaps the best description came from Phil Johnson, the coach of the Kansas City Kings.

"If you had to mold a player," said Johnson, "and say, this is the perfect center, it would be Kareem. He has the stamina and mental attitude to go with speed and agility. Who stops him? No man alive. You just have to play position—and pray."

Reed was stronger than Abdul-Jabbar, but not as big. Russell combined quickness with defense, and Chamberlain was known as the stationary center, more powerful in the basket area, strong on ball handling and muscle. But Abdul-Jabbar is the "moving pivot," with the speed and finesse of a forward.

"Kareem does more things to help win games," Newell said. "There isn't a center in the N.B.A. who passes and steals the ball as well as he does. It's difficult to conceive of anybody being any quicker. He literally explodes, especially when he gets upset. He does not allow himself a mediocre performance. Nobody in the league puts more effort into playing both ends of the floor than he does."

Most centers, coming downcourt, don't move the way guards and forwards do; they are only about half as active. But Abdul-Jabbar moves from the high and low posts outside the basket, from one side of the lane to the other. When he has to, he even brings the ball down. He exerts far more energy than most big men. Even when he gets the ball in the post, he uses moves and not just muscle.

Once while coming downcourt, in a game against the Knicks, Abdul-Jabbar paused to go after the dribbling Walt Frazier. It was astounding to observers that a player of his height would attempt to flick the ball out of the hands of an artist like Frazier. But Kareem has the agility to try tricks like that—and succeed.

"He could be the first seven-foot-plus backcourt man," Fred Crawford, who grew up with Kareem in New York and later was his teammate with the Bucks, once said. "He can dribble and make moves no big man ever made before. Bill Russell could dribble straight down the floor, but Kareem can bring up the ball and handle it. He fakes you, and no man his size could do that.

"He has the best aspects of Russell and Chamberlain in one ball player. Kareem has all Russell's quickness. Offensively, he's a better shot than Wilt Chamberlain, and he moves. Wilt used to go into the post and lean on people, and when he did, there wasn't much you could do about it. Kareem beats you with speed and agility, and he has more shots than Chamberlain."

Abdul-Jabbar cuts so imposing a figure on the court that he has had a profound influence on basketball. While he was still a student at Power Memorial Academy in Manhattan, his potential to dominate the game threw a fright into the National Collegiate Athletic Association. It legislated against the use of the dunk shot, but restored it for the 1976-77 season. Long before Kareem's graduation from U.C.L.A., the N.B.A. widened the center lanes from 12 to 16 feet and banned offensive goal-tending.

"The rule changes have helped Kareem," Newell said. "When Wilt was growing up, the lanes were narrow and he could camp himself underneath the basket. With the widened key areas, it wasn't so much a center's game. Since Kareem had to shoot further away from the basket, he developed more shots, including the greatest hook in the game."

Kareem officially began his pro career by winning the tip from Walt Bellamy. Eighteen seconds later, he had his first field goal, scoring on a set play. He took a pass in the pivot, made a move to his left, and hit in a turnaround jumper from 12 feet out—as the crowd roared its approval.

Three and a half minutes later, with Milwaukee ahead, 10-9, Kareem hit on a pair of layups in quick succession. Twice in the next ensuing four minutes, Detroit forged ahead, but each time Abdul-Jabbar's hook shots regained the lead.

The Bucks led, 60-53, at halftime, and Kareem had scored 19 points, grabbed six rebounds and had two assists. But his most spectacular move of the game that Milwaukee won, 119-110, came in the second quarter.

Kareem swept across the court to his left and put in a left-handed hook, holding the ball on his fingertips and hanging in midair for what appeared to be seconds before he released the ball. The shot was disallowed. He had been charged with an offensive foul.

After the game, Jack Twyman, the ABC color man, was saying, "This could be the start of big things in Milwaukee. Kareem plays like Bill Russell, but he's a better shooter. Beyond his shooting, I was impressed with the way he made the Bucks move. His ability to hit the open man is amazing. He's a complete ball player and a very unselfish one."

After playing the full 48 minutes, scoring 29 points, grabbing 12 rebounds, handing off for six assists, and blocking three shots, and generally intimidating any Pistons who ventured near the basket, Kareem continued to prove himself a perfectionist.

"I don't care too much for my play," the overpowering giant said. "I made a lot of mistakes and took some bad shots."

Mistakes or no mistakes, the national television audience, and the 7,782 fans in the Milwaukee arena that day, saw the birth of pro basketball's next superstar.

As the season progressed, Abdul-Jabbar made fewer mistakes and took more and more good shots.

Finally, came the matchup that the nation's basketball fans had waited for—Kareem Abdul-Jabbar versus Wilt Chamberlain of the Los Angeles Lakers. Again, Kareem was disappointed with his first showing against Wilt. Although, the two giants of basketball put on a dazzling display, Chamberlain scored 25 points, two less than Kareem, and grabbed 25 rebounds to Abdul-Jabbar's 20.

"I learned a few things that night," Kareem admitted after the game. "I was just a skinny kid out there and he was the master."

Chamberlain was later to injure his knee, not playing for the rest of the season.

As the long N.B.A. season progressed, Kareem improved with every passing day.

"I was worried at first that I wouldn't be strong enough to last through that long season," Kareem said. "But I used weights and I tried to build up my strength. I didn't want to get too heavy because I wouldn't have my quickness. But Bill Russell never weighed a lot. He was skinny and he made it through all those years. I decided that if he could do it, so could I."

When the season was over, Kareem had transformed the Bucks from dismal cellar-dwellers into a team that finished second in the Eastern Division with a 56-26 won-lost record. Abdul-Jabbar was voted the rookie of the year. His 2,361 points (a 28.8 scoring average), was the second-best rookie performance behind Jerry West's as a Los Angeles Laker. He was also third in the league in rebounding, with a 14.5 average.

Moreover, he had done wonders for the Milwaukee franchise. The Buck attendance increased 3,000 more a game over the previous season, despite a two-dollar raise in ticket prices. Stock in the Milwaukee Bucks— traded over the counter—shot up from $5 to $12 a share.

In Kareem's rookie season the Bucks reached the Eastern Division final against the Knicks, who went on to win the N.B.A. championship. On April 21, 1970, twenty-four hours after their elimination by New York, the Bucks stunned the rest of the league with the acquisition of the redoubtable Oscar Robertson from the Cincinnati Royals. The teaming of the Big O and the Big A was the prelude to the Bucks winning the 1970-71 championship.

Basketball is a game of feints and fakes, and advantages are often gained in a player's first step past an opponent. Robertson had the reputation of being a complete player, one who could not be stereotyped. He had complete physical control of his body, and there was no one aspect to his greatness. He was good overall. He could keep his balance to an exceptional degree, change direction in midair, and coordinate lighteninglike reflexes.

During Kareem's rookie season, Costello had viewed opponents' ability to swoop in the double- and triple-team Abdul-Jabbar. With the acquisition of Robertson, something the Buck coach termed "a marriage made in heaven," the Bucks coach said. "The other teams won't be able to sag on Kareem and forget everybody else."

Costello had developed an attack that suited Robertson. It was designed to keep men in motion. And from the start of the season, the Bucks wheeled off each other into the lane for quick pops, or went back-door for layups.

Robertson made Kareem—who had already matured some, grown stronger, and learned a lot more about the pro game—into an even more awesome player. Oscar had also provided the Bucks with the poise and leadership that made for an exciting season, giving Milwaukee the kind of attention it had not enjoyed since the late 1950s when the Milwaukee Braves had dominated baseball's National League.

The Bucks won a then league record 20 straight games and finished the regular season with 66 victories and 16 defeats. Milwaukee also established league marks for the most victories at home (34), the most on the road (28), field goal percentage (.509), field goals (3,927), and assists (2,249). Abdul-Jabbar won the scoring title with a 31.7 average and was selected the N.B.A.'s most valuable player.

The Bucks were equally devastating during the playoffs. They beat the San Francisco Warriors and the Los Angeles Lakers, each in a five-game series, and then overwhelmed the Baltimore Bullets in four straight games, only the second time in league history that such a sweep had been accomplished.

After six seasons with Bucks, Kareem, unhappy playing in Milwaukee, forced a trade to the Los Angeles Lakers for the 1975-76 season. But whether he wore the uniform of the Milwaukee Bucks or that of the Lakers, Abdul-Jabbar continued his domination of the game. Even though the Lakers failed to make the playoffs in his first season in Los Angeles, Kareem was still voted the league's most-valuable-player award for the fourth time. In his second season with the Lakers, Kareem led Los Angeles to the Pacific Division title and the best won-lost record in the N.B.A. He was again named the M.V.P., his fifth such award, equaling the record held by Bill Russell. But there were still a lot of playing days left for Kareem Abdul-Jabbar.

# 12

# Willis Reed—the Gentle Giant

A STROLL THROUGH the Madison Square Garden
Hall of Fame Club awakens memories of Hank
Luisetti's one-handed jump shot that revolutionized
college basketball, Wilt Chamberlain's 100- and 73-
point games against the Knicks, and Ernie Calverley's
20-foot shot at the buzzer in the 1946 National Invitation Tournament. There are also memories of Bob Pettit's feats, and the way Bill Russell glamorized defense
as a Boston Celtic.

But nowhere in the Hall of Fame Club or the
Naismith Memorial Hall of Fame at Springfield, Massachusetts, can anyone recapture the emotion Willis
Reed stirred at Madison Square Garden on May 8,
1970, in the seventh game of the N.B.A. championship
series between the New York Knicks and the Los Angeles Lakers.

Four days earlier, with almost four minutes left in

the first quarter of the fifth game of the series, Reed lay twisted on the Garden floor after an attempt to drive on Wilt Chamberlain. The action moved upcourt as Willis writhed in pain at the other end of the floor. Reed hobbled back into action for one more sequence of plays before he left the game, no longer able to withstand the pain of the injured right hip.

As he limped out of the huge arena to a standing ovation, the Garden was quickly transformed from a rollicking funhouse into a hospital waiting room.

"I was sick inside when I saw Willis," said Dave De-Busschere.

DeBusschere understood that of the two teams trying to win the N.B.A. championship, the Knicks were suddenly second. "You never give up," added Dave, "but inside you knew your chances were very slim."

Reed had played a decisive role in every playoff game the Knicks had won. But without the 6-foot-9-inch, 240-pound center to intimidate and battle Chamberlain under the boards, the Lakers raced off to a 53-40 lead at halftime.

During the intermission, each normal movement by Reed sent spears dancing along the *rectis femorus*, the big, overworked muscle which most of the Knicks had never heard of before their captain's injury.

The rest of the game was one of those melodramas that turns a sports arena into a theatre, as the Knicks, with the hlep of 19 second-half Los Angeles turnovers and only 26 attempted shots, made up for the loss of Reed with a gambling defense that stunned the Lakers.

Walt Frazier, the Knick backcourt man who had scored 21 points, called the 107-100 victory that gave New York a 3-2 lead in the series, "unreal." But everyone agreed that it was a triumph for Willis Reed.

As the Knicks picked up all over the court and double-teamed the ball with the ferocity of men who had lost all reason, Reed lay on the training table in the dressing room as a doctor worked on his hip. He listened to the account of the game on the public-address system the club had piped into the dressing room.

"I was excited," Reed said. "All I could do was root. I was taking treatment and all I could do was be a fan. When we won, it sounded like a fantasy. It was one of the most inspiring moments of my life."

DeBusschere was later to say that Red Holzman, the Knick coach, had told the players, "Let's win this one for Willis. He's won a lot of games for us. Let's win one for him."

The next day after Xrays and further examinations, Reed left for California with the Knicks with little optimism that he would be able to play in the sixth game. Through most of the flight he lay sprawled and slumped in a middle-aisle seat. Occasionally he dozed. During most of the flight, there was the look of private agony and pain on his face.

Soon after their arrival in Los Angeles, Reed and Danny Whalen, the trainer, went to the Century Plaza Hotel Health Club. As part of its facilities, the health club had a huge ten-jet whirlpool bath. Willis sat in the warm whirlpool for a while, plunged into a tank of ice-cold water, and then entered the steaming sauna bath. Afterwards, it was back to the whirlpool to start another round.

For two hours he subjected his pain-wracked body to this routine. The next morning he returned to the health club again. This time he spent four hours soaking, steaming, and freezing the damaged muscle. But it was all to no avail. Reed sat out the sixth game and

Chamberlain, virtually uncontested, demolished the Knicks, 135-113, pulling down 27 rebounds and scoring 45 points.

Then, suddenly, it was Friday, the day of the seventh and final game. For dyed-in-the-wool Knick fans, it was the 1,858th game, completing twenty-four years of frustration.

For most of the afternoon, Reed had undergone rigorous therapy treatments. Then, following a meal and telephone calls to his mother in Bernice, Louisiana and his daughter Veronica, celebrating her fifth birthday, Reed returned to the dressing room for heat treatments at 5 P.M. But even after a shot of cortisone it was still doubtful whether he would play.

Shortly after 6 P.M., Reed, in uniform, walked slowly onto the Garden floor, followed by teammate Donny May, who came with him to snag the rebounds. Slowly and deliberately, Reed moved around the floor, throwing up soft one-handers. He did not jump, nor would he acknowledge his pain.

More than an hour later, Phil Jackson left the Knick dressing room. His skin had a greenish look. On his face was a grimace.

"The needle was that long," said Phil, his hands a half-foot apart.

Jackson was talking about the instrument used for two injections of cortisone and carbocaine, the pain-killers that Dr. James Parkes had shoved into Reed's right thigh.

At 7:34 P.M. Willis Reed stopped being just the captain of the Knicks, plus the most valuable player in the N.B.A. All-Star game and during the regular season.

As he walked through the entranceway, his face

grim, Willis Reed—born June 25, 1942 in Hico, Louisiana, a place he says was so tiny "they don't even have a population"—became more than a sports hero or a national magazine cover boy. From the moment he walked onto the court to join in the warmup, it was no longer a basketball game, but a crusade. It was a vendetta of emotion.

Reed, who once picked cotton "to buy myself a pair of shoes," was cheered wildly by his teammates, by newspaper reporters and editors, who are not supposed to show any emotions, by Dustin Hoffman, the movie star, and by people young and old in the capacity crowd of 19,500, many with tear-filled eyes. They applauded, they whistled, they cheered the courage of Willis Reed.

"It all came at exactly the right moment," said Bill Bradley. "We were high when we came out to warm up; we settled down toward the end of the warmup. Then he came out, got that ovation, and it brought us up sky-high."

In less than two minutes after the start of the game, Reed hit on two jump shots that gave the Knicks a 5-2 lead, an advantage they never lost. Walt Frazier scored 36 points and tied a playoff record of 19 assists, shared jointly by Bob Cousy when he played for the Boston Celtics, and Chamberlain.

Statistics and adjectives cannot convey the all-around effort by DeBusschere in the 113-99 victory. Obtained from the Detroit Pistons on December 19, 1968 as the final figure in the Knick championship design, DeBusschere gave a magnificent demonstration of hustling, rebounding, shotting, tipping, and playing defense every inch of the 96-foot court. He scored 18 points and grabbed 17 rebounds.

Reed knew what *he* had to do: outmaneuver Wilt Chamberlain. He kept Chamberlain from doing what he wanted to do. If Wilt wanted a spot on the floor to set up, Reed denied him that spot. He forced the 7-1 Laker center further away from the basket than he wanted to station himself. And furthermore, Reed did it all on a gimpy leg.

Reed, voted the M.V.P., played only 27 minutes, but what a 27 minutes! And that was the needed therapy, not only for Willis, who never was so scared, but for the Knicks, who went off on a classic basketball trip to their first championship, taking the wild, incredulous fans with them.

During the celebration, as champagne flowed freely, DeBusschere expressed himself without saying a word. He elbowed his way through a mass of reporters, reached down, grabbed Willis Reed's arm, and pulled the aching captain to his feet. Then he threw his arms around him and they embraced. They were more than teammates; they were brothers.

In another part of the dressing room Dave Stallworth stood against the wall, away from the champagne that Nate Bowman was squirting.

"Willis is beautiful, just beautiful," said Stallworth. "To me personally, he showed so much guts, you had to gut it with him. You had to do it, too. You got to go mad when a man who ought to be in a wheelchair comes out there. But if his presence could give us what we needed to win, he had to do it. He's a helluva man."

Willis Reed was a helluva player. He was the heart and soul of the 1969-70 team—at times called the best ever assembled on one basketball court. Opposing players often said that without Reed, the Knicks were just an ordinary team.

Reed was a master at setting "picks" for his teammates. They were beautiful and they were jarring, even against the taller and heavier players. They were unshakable, and every Knick scored behind them.

In the season that followed the championship, tendonitis began to plague Reed's left knee. Although he played in seventy-three games during the 1970-71 season, and averaged 20.9 points, his condition had deteriorated badly by playoff time. He averaged only 12 points a game, and the Knicks were beaten in the Eastern Division semifinal by the Baltimore Bullets.

After the season, Reed underwent surgery on the aching knee. His rehabilitation continued throughout the summer and into the training camp. "But through it all, I knew something wasn't right," Willis said. "It kept hurting all the time. They said the surgery had been successful, but all I knew was it still hurt."

In the early weeks of the 1971-72 season, his playing time was sporadic. On November 11, after the first half in a game against the Golden State Warriors, Reed gave up. The pain was too great. In the months that followed he sat in street clothes first on the Knick bench, and then at the scorers' table, unable to play again that season.

Reed's frustration grew, when critics speculated that he would never be back.

On September 22, 1972, seconds before the first quarter of a preseason game against the Bullets ended, Reed snapped the switch off a heating pad on his left knee. Danny Whalen put some eyewash in Willis' eyes. Reed was being readied for his first performance in more than ten months.

The standing-room crowd of 2,500 at Monmouth (N.J.) College cheered Reed's appearance, just as they had in the pregame introductions when John Condon, the Garden announcer, said, "Let's welcome back the captain, number nineteen, Willis Reed."

Four days later the Knicks' exhibition season moved to the Garden. There, the ovation grew even more tumultuous for the man New York had come to know not only as a great athlete, but as a man of intense pride and dedication to his goals.

During the 1972-73 season, newspaper headlines read: REED MAKES HIS PRESENCE FELT, IT WAS AN ENCOURAGING EVENING FOR WILLIS, REED'S MOVING UP, WILLIS IS JUST A JUMP AWAY, WILLIS IS READY, THIS TIME WILLIS WINS THE BATTLE, TURNING POINT FOR WILLIS, THE RETURN OF THE ENFORCER, FOR REED IT'S PARADISE REGAINED.

Finally, on May 11, 1973, the headline read: WILLIS GETS IT BACK. "It" was no less than N.B.A. championship, and Willis Reed was named the most valuable player in the final playoff series against the Los Angeles Lakers.

Since the doctors had immobilized his leg in a cast for six months and advised him to forget about playing, Reed had come a long way. During that time, everybody was an expert on the subject of the future of Willis Reed. Everyone had an opinion. And most opinions were that his basketball career was at an end.

On May 15, 1973, Reed stood on the dais of a New York restaurant and received another standing ovation from a cheering audience. Memories of the headlines that chronicled his progress from October 1972 through May 1973, plus all the agony and the pain, must have raced through his mind.

At that luncheon, in honor of his being selected the series M.V.P., this gentle giant of a man said, "My momma told me I could come back from my injury. What momma says is right."

Later, Reed was to say, "I never had any doubt I'd play again. Even when I couldn't play and run, I lived in the hope and had faith in the doctors. They had assured me the program they gave me would do it. All I had to do was work at it.

"I knew that time was in my favor. The more I played, the more beneficial it would be ... and it worked out that way. I was surprised it took that long."

During the course of that "long time," the legion of Reed doubters grew. They took note of his slow return to form, the games he looked old in, and the nagging injuries.

The critics said he was hurting the team, that he had lost his rhythm, timing, and movement. They forgot that Reed was coming back after a full year's absence from the game. They overlooked the fact that his slow return had to do with his surgical knee. They were impatient; Willis was not.

A few nights before that luncheon, the sweat poured off Reed's huge, 240-pound brown body as he sat in a tumultuous Knick dressing room in the Los Angeles Forum. The Knicks had just beaten the Lakers for the fourth straight time after an opening loss in the final seven-game championship playoff series.

Reed was a mountain of strength, and the Knicks relied on him heavily to minimize Wilt Chamberlain's defensive threat. Additionally, he scored 18 points, grabbed 12 rebounds, and had 7 assists.

"I really forgot how good Willis was," said Bill Bradley, the scholarly Knick, that night. "Two years of struggling, all kinds of pressure, it's phenomenal."

As Reed slowly removed the tape from his legs and accepted congratulations for the M.V.P. honors, he let it be known that a part of the honor was meant for "the man." The man was Red Holzman, the Knick coach.

"Red took his time with me," said Willis. "He knew what I was going through. I was suffering. I wasn't able to be consistent."

Holzman said, "I don't think he's all the way back. People tend to forget how really good he was in the old days. But he's the type of guy who's very determined. He was determined to come back. There were days and nights when it was very tough. He'd get to a certain level and fall back. But he kept coming back."

Reed and the Knick championships have been intertwined. New York's franchise, buried deep in the N.B.A. cellar for nine seasons, began to turn around only after his arrival for the 1964-65 season. The Knicks have won only two championships in their thirty-year history. Both times Reed was the inspiration, playing some of his finest games.

There is more to Reed the person than the hulking 6-9 figure that used to clog the middle, set picks, grab rebounds, score, and play defense. There was, for example, the time in 1970, the first season of the new Cleveland franchise. The Cavaliers had lost their 33rd game in 35 outings in a comedy of errors.

After one game, when they had kicked the ball around, passed loosely, and done everything but play pro basketball, they were subject to some kibitzing by the New York players, spectators, and sportswriters.

Willis listened sympathetically. He had the compassion to understand the point of view of the loser.

"I remember when the Knicks used to lose," said Reed at the time. "When you have been that way yourself, you appreciate how tough it can be. Some guys in this league came right out and joined winning teams and they don't understand a loser."

He understood because the Knicks had finished in the Eastern Division cellar in his first two years.

After they had made Reed their second-round draft choice out of Grambling College, there was no way to put dollar value on what he meant to the Knicks during his ten seasons. He gave his soul to the New York franchise, and the magic name of Willis Reed became the primary reason why the Knick ticket used to be the hottest and most difficult to come by.

Actually, Reed fit no mold. Any effort to describe him would echo the best clichés a press agent has to offer. In these days, when sports are defined in dollar signs, it's difficult to use words like "gentle," "kind-hearted," "proud," "dignified," "aristocratic," and "honorable," words that best described Willis Reed, the Knick.

One need only ask Eddie Donovan, his first Knick coach, or Mrs. Cora Alcindor, the mother of Kareem Abdul-Jabbar of the Los Angeles Lakers, and they will sing the praises of Willis.

Donovan, the Knick general manager, will tell you that when he called out Reed's name in the 1964 draft, the franchise got something special.

"I'll never forget that day," recalled Donovan. "It was after our first practice session that there was a knock at the door. It was Willis asking to borrow a rule book. He wanted to know what he could do and couldn't do. I had never heard of a player, any player, asking for a rule book before."

Mrs. Alcindor will tell you she disliked it when Willis muscled her son, but she praised him for his help in her work for charity.

Every time he speaks of Reed or is in his presence, there is a gleam in the eyes of Fred Hodby, his coach at Grambling. "He has never forgotten Grambling," said Hodby, "and I don't suppose he ever will. He is that kind of person."

In his book *The Open Man*, Dave DeBusschere called Reed "our one indispensable man." And Bradley said, "Willis' leadership is substance, not a myth. Sometimes leadership is not perceived even by the people who are being led. Willis has perceived leadership."

After the 1973-74 season, the pain and the prospect of further knee surgery forced Reed into early retirement. He left behind a mark of 12,183 regular season points, 8,414 rebounds, and a legion of memories.

Testimony to his never-fogotten popularity always surfaces when he often returned to watch the Knicks play. On such nights, John Condon, the Garden P.A. announcer, would say, "In our audience is an old friend, Willis Reed. Let's welcome him back."

Suddenly, there would be a standing ovation and for many in the crowd it was May 8, 1970, or May 10, 1973, all over again.

At the start of the 1976-77 season, the Knicks set a precedent and retired Reed's jersey number 19 in a special pregame ceremony. It was the first uniform the team had ever retired.

Before the season was over Mike Burke, president of the Knicks, stood before more than a hundred members of the news media and announced, "The captain has become the coach."

For Willis Reed was named to succeed Holzman as the Knick coach, effective with the 1977-78 season.

# 13

# Eight Unforgettable Days In May

KEITH WILKES, the newly named National Basketball Association rookie of the year, burst into the Golden State Warrior dressing room at the Capital Center, and shouted, "We're Champions of the World!" Al Attles, the coach, grabbed him by the hand and together they danced a jig. There were songs and boisterous laughter and champagne showers that Sunday afternoon, May 25, 1975, in Landover, Maryland. But for Rick Barry, there were also tears.

Barry, bone-weary and sweat-drenched, had his head buried in his hands. He was crying unashamedly. Cliff Ray, the Warriors' towering center, stopped celebrating when he noticed his captain sitting alone on the bench near his locker. He walked over and patted Barry softly on the head. Barry didn't look up. Ten years of professional basketball frustration had welled up inside him, bursting out in a flood of tears.

139

He had been called traitor, money-hungry, arrogant, cry-baby, selfish, temperamental, and moody. Now he had been named the most valuable player in the play-offs. Suddenly they were calling him the greatest player in the NBA, the man who had taken the underdog Warriors to four straight, stunning victories over the Washington Bullets for the 1974-75 championship.

The young Warriors, with the irrepressible Barry and seven players each with three years' experience or less, given no chance of getting into the playoffs before the season began, had completed eight unforgettable days in May. It was only the third four-game sweep in the 29-year NBA playoff history. Only the 1959 Boston Celtics and the 1971 Milwaukee Bucks had accomplished the feat before.

The Warriors had played hard ball throughout the championship series the Bullets were supposed to have won handily. They had never panicked, despite their alleged inexperience, and they were decisively better inside, where almost all basketball games are won and lost.

The upset had been witnessed by millions on television and by the thousands who managed to get seats at the Cow Palace in San Francisco and at the Capital Center. They had seen Rick Barry, the perfectionist, at his best, setting up his teammates with pinpoint passing, fighting for loose balls, rebounding, and hustling for baskets. And with every basket, his right arm had shot skyward in a boyishly enthusiastic salute. He was the leader, the inspiration, the superstar on the top-to-bottom team of "no names."

In the seventeen games on the road to the championship, Barry scored 470 points, dealt out 103 assists, and grabbed 94 rebounds. He also made 50 steals during the playoffs, eight of them against the Seattle SuperSonics—both league records—and walked away with a flock of accolades.

Jeff Mullins, now a television announcer but at the time a Warrior backcourtman, recalling the final game a year later, said, "The biggest miracle to me was still the last four minutes, when we were losing by eight points. I played the entire fourth quarter and thought to myself there was sure to be a fifth game. Then the Bullets started throwing the ball away. We threw it away almost as much, but we got closer and then went ahead. The last minute and a half was a comedy of errors. We got the ball with one second to go, ahead by one point because Butch Beard had made the last of three free throws."

When Barry finally regained his composure and joined his teammates in the victory celebration, he said, "We made reality out of fantasy. This was the most rewarding season I've ever had. We were supposed to be a run-of-the-mill team, but instead of the Bullets beating us four straight, we beat them four straight. It was tremendous. Everything fell into place. It was really a fantasy kind of year, the type of season that you dream about, but doesn't happen."

Throughout the celebration, a parade of rival coaches jammed the dressing room congratulating Al Attles and praising Barry.

Tom Heinsohn, the Boston Celtics' coach, called Barry "the best all-around player in the game." And another coach said, "I don't think I've seen Barry play better basketball than he did this season. He did everything, and through his example, the other players followed his lead. Don't forget most of them were new to the team. Nobody gave them a tumble when the season opened, and now they are the champions."

This was the same Rick Barry who had left behind a trail of friends and critics as he traveled from the N.B.A. to the American Basketball Association and back to the N.B.A.—five different teams in ten seasons of fun, pain, and legal maneuvers. At times it appeared he had spent as much time in the courts as on them. Lawsuits pursued him in the A.B.A. sites of Oakland, Washington, Virginia, and New York. He was under contract to two teams at the same time, and only a court order forced him back to the Golden State Warriors from the New York Nets.

Over the years, he had been bad-mouthed on the east and west coasts and booed in between. He had been accused of shooting the ball too much and showing an indifference to playing defense. Even before Barry had turned pro, there were those who said he was "flaky," a cry-baby, that he didn't have the muscle or the fight to make it in the N.B.A.

The federal courts had ripped away his Nets uniform three years before (1972) and Barry, suffering yet another crushing setback, had vowed to retire. But as the unpredictable and controversial Barry had done so often since 1965, he changed his mind when the Warriors, who had been his first pro team, offered a reported 3-year, $1.6-million contract.

Now he was walking through the dressing room at the Capital Center, his eyes wet and red, and congratulating the teammates who had placed their faith in him. He hugged Derrek Dickey, a no-name who had led all the shooters in the championship series, and who had done a good defensive job on Washington's Elvin Hayes.

"My man," said Derrek and together they laughed and sipped champagne. Then he turned to Steve Bracey, the twelfth man on Rick Barry's no-name team, and Bracey laughed and poured champagne on Barry's head. "I'll take it, I'll take it," said Barry and they laughed and hugged. Cliff Ray, who came to the Warriors at the start of the season in a deal for Nate Thurmond, wiped the champagne off Barry's face.

The team that played together, worked together, stuck together, and won together was now celebrating together, with teamwork. Coach Al Attles was talking to the television people; Joe Roberts, his assistant who took charge on the bench after Attles had been ejected by the officials in the opening minutes of the championship clincher, was talking to writers; Bill Bridges, who had earned his first N.B.A. championship ring in twelve years of professional basketball, was hugging Charley Johnson, the no-name of the backcourt; Phil Smith and Charlie Dudley, the other backcourt no-names, were guzzling champagne like veterans.

Barry characterized the Warriors, when he finally found his voice, "as one of the most unique teams in all of basketball history. A time that cares for each other. The most beautiful individuals I've ever been associated with. I don't know how anyone can top it. The championship is everything. I never thought at the beginning of the year we could achieve it. This team has character. This is the most rewarding thing, the happiest thing that's ever happened to me. It's everything. I only wish I was in a position to retire now."

The man who had been equally vilified and regaled for his activities on and off the court, lifted the champagne glass and took a long drink as the sweat and champagne ran down his 6-foot 7-inch frame. At the same time, the boy in Barry recalled how his father would shout to him as he practiced running backwards, "Get back. Don't look at the ball when you dribble." He remembered those nights in the gym at the University of Miami when he would practice alone, sometimes past midnight, and how his teammates used to scoff at him.

Now, in his third season with the Warriors since his return from the Nets, the longest one-town stint of his professional career, Barry could no longer be called a superstar who couldn't help a team win a championship. Barry had matured. This year he hadn't got caught up in helpless arguments with officials as he had so many times before.

He had actively campaigned to become the team captain before the season began, and amazed even himself by his conduct. Barry had changed. He took another long drink of the sparkling wine.

He had not even drawn a technical foul in the entire playoffs. "It took me ten years to realize you can't win an argument with an official," he said. Even when Mike Riordan of the Bullets had tried to draw him into a fight early in the fourth game of the championship series, Barry had managed to avert trouble.

Barry, who had averaged 30.6 points during the regular season—second only to Bob McAdoo—had been matched with the 6-4 Riordan in the three regular season games. Mike, who had grown from a twelfth-round draft pick to become one of the N.B.A.'s outstanding small forwards, had clearly won the regular-season battle against Barry. He limited Rick to eight points in one of the meetings and held his average against the Bullets to 16.3 points. In the one game Riordan had missed, Barry scored 34.

Pro basketball is clearly a game of matchups, and even before the Golden State-Washington final series had opened, the Barry-Riordan matchup had been considered one of the key factors. But when it was all over, Barry left no doubt that he was the master in the first three playoff games. Then, three minutes into the final game, Riordan precipitated a fight and was charged with a foul, as Barry coolly walked away.

"I amazed myself at my restraint," Barry said.

Riordan denied that he had attempted to get Barry involved, and perhaps ejected from the game, and insisted instead that he was simply playing "aggressive" basketball. A younger Barry might have fallen for the ploy and fought Riordan, but this year it was *Captain* Barry. He had his team to think about. He let Coach Attles fight those battles.

The Washington Bullets had gambled on the playoff schedule, but it didn't seem to matter. The original setup called for the first two games to be played on the Bullets' home court, the next two in Oakland, and the remaining games to be alternated. Then it was discovered that the Ice Follies had been previously booked to play the Coliseum.

Who had expected the Warriors still to be playing basketball in May?

Franklin Mieuli, the Warrior owner, had the perfect answer after his team had won the opener, 101-95. "Like Phoenix," he said, "we have risen from the ashes."

With Barry scoring 36 points, Golden State rushed back from a 13-point deficit and won the second game, 92-91, as Washington missed two shots in the final six seconds. The Warriors made it 3-0 by winning, 109-101.

Toward the end of the third game, the Bullets, whose coach, K.C. Jones, had learned about playoff pressures as a Boston Celtic, looked harassed and disorganized. Washington was manhandled by Barry, who got 38 points, and by George Johnson, subbing for Cliff Ray, who added ten points and grabbed nine rebounds.

Before the fourth game, Wes Unseld of the Bullets was to say, "It's very important that we get a couple of victories even if we lose the series. We need it for the future. For next year, for our state of mind."

The Warriors had battered the Bullets on the boards, even though Washington's front line included Wes Unseld, the league's top rebounder, and Elvin Hayes. Golden State also succeeded in choking off the running game.

"We led the league in rebounding," said Al Attles, "something few people seem to remember. Maybe that's because we didn't have the one big-name rebounder. Instead, we had eight guys getting eight rebounds each. Sometimes I think that when a team has one big rebounder, there is a tendency for everyone else to stand around."

The Warriors came from behind in almost every playoff game, and much of their success can be credited to Attles' coaching style in the early days of the regular season. He sent in his players in waves, and they outhustled and outscrambled the opposition. It was no different against the Bullets.

"We went at them twelve different ways," said Attles. "They didn't know who was going to do what, or what to expect from whom."

While Attles was making use of all his players, K.C. Jones primarily countered with six. And the sixth man,

Nick Weatherspoon, a forward, after a torrid 59 percent floor shooting against Buffalo and Boston in the earlier playoff rounds, failed to hit even 20 percent in the final. In the first three games the Warrior reserves had outscored the Bullet reserves, 115-53.

"If you expect people to play for you in the playoffs," Attles said, "you have to play them in some critical spots during the season and hope they're ready. They have to be ready mentally, and fundamentals are important to this sport. That's not something you can turn on like a water faucet.

"The lack of recognition given some of the players, and the team as a whole, bothered me. People tended to overlook us completely, but I'm not going to argue about what people think."

Why should he, or any of the Golden State Warriors, be concerned? They divided $330,500 in playoff money, for beating the Bullets, not bad for a team that was ridiculed before the season began.

And during the summer when Barry, the celebrity, wasn't making money, he had time to reflect on that championship season.

"After we beat the Bullets in the first two games, I could see it begin to happen," he said. "Our guys began to get that dazed look in their eyes. The Bullets' faces went from expressions of smug confidence to masks of fear and disbelief.

"I recently got a chance to watch for the first time some game films of the fourth and final game with Washington," said Barry. "Looking back on it now, it seems like a case of destiny. Wes Unseld gets a rebound and for no reason it bounces off his knee out of bounds. Dick Gibbs misses an uncontested lay-in and we win the game. Fate played a major role." And with a smile and a pause he added, "as did the coaching of Al Attles."

The Golden State fans had cut down the nets after each of the first three Warriors' triumphs in the championship series, but after the fourth and clinching victory, they stole owner Franklin Mieuli's hat and broke through police lines at San Francisco International Airport in celebration.

"We're number one! we're number one!" an exuberant crowd of 3,000 chanted after they had waited up to five hours for their heroes' return from Landover. When the team finally showed up, it was by taxi.

A minor malfunction had forced their plane to land in Oakland, California, and the management had decided to reward the noisy fans by bringing the Warriors across the bay by taxi anyway. The crowd had to be restrained by the cordon of police until they caught sight of their heroes. Who knows how long they might have waited, had the Warriors not shown up at the airport!

Sixty San Mateo County sheriff's deputies and airport police stood by helplessly as the fans surged past the policemen, swarming over cabs for a better look at the Warriors. Police said it was the biggest airport crowd to greet a local sports team since the San Francisco Giants returned home with the 1962 National League pennant.

The fans waved signs that read: "Go Warriors Go" and "Only the Warriors do things right in Washington." The four-game sweep was considered the biggest sports upset of the year.

When Rick Barry finally got his chance to address the crowd, he said, "They said we would fold, but the Bullets were the ones who folded."

The fans responded by wildly cheering. No one had expected the Warriors to be taking the cheers from the crowd. The preseason prognosticators had picked Golden State to finish fourth in the five-team Pacific Division.

Meanwhile, Mieuli scanned the airport crowd for his stolen checkered deerstalker cap.

"It was my security blanket," he said. "I don't know why anyone else would want it. It was really soggy. Rick Barry had soaked it with champagne twice after the final game."

Mieuli offered a substantial reward for the return of the hat.

"Whoever has it," he begged, "can have a ride on my boat, season tickets to the Warrior games next year, a ride on my motorcycle, and a lot of love."

Mieuli, one of the few remaining one-man N.B.A. ownerships, had waited a long time for the celebration. For years his Warriors had been losers, especially at the box office. He had tossed good money after bad, and had been maligned for doing it. For years his franchise had played second fiddle to the Los Angeles Lakers. It was always the Los Angeles Lakers this and the Los Angeles Lakers that.

But winning the championship was the cure-all. The Barry-led team, shorn of other stars, studded with rookies and upgraded reserves, had soared the average attendance from a measly 2,000 to over 10,000.

When Barry had walked into the 1974 training camp, his initial reaction was that he was to be the link with the past in a rebuilding season. There was no reason to dispute that reaction.

The names on the Warrior roster were conspicuous for their anonymity—Phil Smith, Charles Dudley, Derrick Dickey, Clifford Ray, Charley Johnson, and Steve Bracey.

Dudley, a guard, had been doing graduate work at the University of Washington the year before, playing pickup games at the gym. The Warriors had drafted him in 1972, then waived him, and he had signed with Seattle, where he was out after twelve games.

Smith? A rookie guard from the University of San Francisco. Derrick Dickey? A second-year forward out of Cincinnati. Johnson had been a sixth-round draft choice from the University of California in 1971. Bracey was a third-year pro from Tulsa by way of the Atlanta Hawks.

A sportswriter stopped Phil Smith in the dressing room once and asked, "Who are you?"

"What?" Smith asked.

"Who are you? I mean, if you had to introduce yourself to the American public, what would you say?"

Smith thought a moment, "Well, I'd say, 'Hi, I'm Phil Smith from the University of San Francisco.'"

The Warriors were young. Barry and the 32-year-old Jeff Mullins had a combined total of eighteen pro seasons, and the rest of the Warriors had logged only fifteen in all. For the final fifteen games of the regular season, 36-year-old Bill Bridges joined the team.

From the old guard, Cazzie Russell had played out his option and signed with the Los Angeles Lakers, and Nate Thurmond, the big, mean and always promising center, was now in Chicago. In return, the Bulls had sent Mieuli some much-needed financial replenishment and 6-9 Cliff Ray with his 8.3 scoring average. There were those on the West Coast who joked that if Ray, standing at the edge of the Coney Island Pier, took ten shots at the water, maybe he would hit on six of them.

"To be honest," said Dick Vertlieb, the general manager, "we traded Thurmond because I needed cash to carry out some other things. We got Ray, but I was just hoping to maintain the team. I didn't think he would improve it. And Dudley—shoot, I was just doing a favor for a friend who suggested we give him another tryout."

In training camp, Attles was to tell his young Warriors, "It's going to be a big change without Thurmond. We're going to miss Clyde Lee, too. We'll have to put in a lot of work to get it together, but it won't be as bad as most people think. I think we'll be all right."

If Attles was playing the role of the optimist, Barry was not.

"I was very pessimistic when we began camp," he said. "It looked as though I was going to finish my career playing on a team trying to rebuild. But after a while when I saw the enthusiasm and the attitude, I became more and more optimistic. I began to feel we'd be competitive."

There is a big difference between being competitive and winning the N.B.A. championship.

For some unexplained reason, the infectious spirit began to take hold, and Barry, looking back at the season, was to say, "This was like a college team. The spirit and enthusiasm were contagious. Nobody cared what we did, or what stars we had. The only thing we cared about was winning."

In the back of everyone's mind was the thought that if the Warriors made it to the 1973-74 playoffs with Thurmond, Russell, and Lee, how could they possibly do it without them?

Attles decided, no matter what, to start Wilkes at forward alongside of Rick Barry. Cliff Ray could make a full-time career of being the big, bad, mean center. The job of scoring points was left to Barry and Wilkes. Thus the pieces slowly began to fall into place.

While the Golden State Warriors were winning the Pacific Division honors with a 48-34 regular-season won-lost record, Attles relied heavily on a backcourt team of Butch Beard, playing for his fourth pro team in five years, and Charley Johnson, a sixth-round draft choice.

"There's a strange chemistry sparking on this team," Al Attles kept telling his friends during the season. "Like something good is about to happen."

After winning the divisional title, they gained momentum as they marched through the playoffs beating the Seattle SuperSonics in six games in the Western Conference semifinal, and the Chicago Bulls in seven games to match them against the Washington Bullets, the Eastern Conference champion. The Bullets had won the regular-season Central Division title and eliminated the Buffalo Braves and the Boston Celtics to gain the final.

Before the start of the championship series against the Bullets, Bill Bridges, who had played on ten playoff teams with the St. Louis and Atlanta Hawks, but had never experienced winning a championship, may have defined the Warrior season best.

"This is a Cinderella team," said Bridges. "It's never going to take the glass slipper off. Sometimes the clock never strikes twelve."